SP.
ARCHAEOLOGY

Practical Shamanism at Sacred Places

FEATURING

SEDONA, ARIZONA

Love & Blessings,
Luminous

Luminous

PORTALS of TRANSCENDENCE
PUBLISHING

PORTALS of TRANSCENDENCE
PUBLISHING
POB 670, Sedona, Arizona 86339
www.PortalsofTranscendence.com

Cover design: Luminous
Art: Luminous, All rights reserved.
Typography: Minion Pro, Bembo Std.

1. travel, spiritual 2. sacred sites and power places 3. archaeology, spiritual
4. spiritual development 5. shamanism

v. 1.0
First Edition
Printed on acid-free paper.

If you are unable to order this book from your local bookseller, you may order directly from the publisher. Email: Portals@esedona.net

I dedicate this book to my beautiful parents, and everyone else who has inspired me, by whatever means, to look more deeply into my Self.

CONTENTS

IV. PRACTICAL SHAMANISM

V. SEDONA, ARIZONA, USA

VI. OUTDOOR AND SITE ETIQUETTE

ACKNOWLEDGMENTS

The writing of this book began inside me, long ago—it has always been going on. Deep and heartfelt thanks and gratitude to everyone who has touched my life. Every relationship experience helped me reach a higher perspective and dive deeper within myself—here are a few: In 1982, Deanna Pedroli told me I should really write down what I was saying—I began carrying a notebook. The San Francisco Art Institute and Multidimensional Dimensional Research and Expansion gave me languages for my experience—visual, emotional, psychic and physical. Jesus Christ and scores of beings, invisible and ever present who help to make the impossible easy. I thank Sherry Bell, Sunday Larson, Bennie Blake and Linda Ingram for their consistent presence and perspectives during the writing process. Sacred sites and power places have inspired and informed me and continue to do so—it was a journey to Peru that initiated this writing.

cast a stone
in the oceans of the past
when time was new
and today was yet to be lived

earth is where the ancestors
planted dreams
at the core of the pyramids
in monuments and myths

ancient glyphs
chiseled loose from stone walls
laid down for memory's sake
reminders of truths
in moments of potential madness

long ago
the ancient ones
scripted a garden of paradise
called planet earth

avatars and ancient gods bartered for time
while spilling dreams like gentle rain
welcoming the spring
the flowering

breath of life activates the sound
stirs stories written upon our bones
stories of this time
that have come to us only in dream time
until now

telepathic language travels
from thought form
into manifestation
faster than the speed of light

homecoming
we are from a world indivisible
a mirror of wholeness
BREATHE

I.
SACRED PLACES

SACRED PLACES

The idea of a sacred place...is apparently as old as life itself.
Joseph Campbell, *The Mythic Image*

Our senses tingle with a curiosity about what lies beyond this physical and visible world, what else exists that we cannot see. The Great Mystery, invisible worlds, ancient and future wisdom, and our intergalactic beginnings remain cloaked in mystery—yet each of us holds a unique piece of this very intricate human puzzle.

The realm of the eternal soul conveys a knowing of the existence of something greater and larger than this life. A goddess, a god, religion, something to believe in, a faith, exceptional wisdom or a being more extraordinary than ourselves, all exist to nourish our need to aspire to something greater. Sacred places have always been the locations and repositories for such yearnings.

Sacred places hold a wealth of information about our hidden history and beginnings, keys to our true nature, and reveal pathways to our future as a species. Archaeology and history continue to revise ideas of the earliest civilizations based on new evidence being found and illuminated. We are much older as a species, have been on the planet longer than our histories tell us, and have created civilizations that are yet to be raised from the dust or the depths of the oceans.

Sacred Places hold the vibration and hidden knowledge of these distant pasts, and it is here that we can reclaim our multidimensional wholeness. Prehistoric civilizations hark back to the time of the gods who were ageless, living thousands of years. They overcame disease and death with the simple breath of life, manifested instantaneously and created for fun.

Sacred places allow spiritual communication—are human freeways to remembrance of our Eternal Divine Self.

Sacred places are certainly part of our collective past and an esteemed part of our Eternal Now. Have you ever thought that your life may be happening in many different places and times, even simultaneously? Have you considered the possibility that our origins and the origins of sacred places are much deeper and older than archaeologists and historians assume from the evidence they uncover? Do you sense there is more going on beneath the surface? Have you ever visited a sacred place as a casual tourist, and found yourself suddenly drawn to explore more deeply? Sacred places are excellent locations to discover the answers to these questions.

What Is a Sacred Place?

Specific planetary locations have been identified as *sacred sites* and *power places*. *Sacred Place(s)* is the term used in this book to identify both. The word *sacred* refers to an extraordinary or unique object, person or place of veneration and awe.

The sacred stands apart from the norm and manifests itself as a reality different from normal realities.

Sacred places have the power to heal, inspire the mind, awaken, clarify, and support the development of psychic abilities. Archaeological sites are not all sacred and sacred places have varying levels of aliveness. Following is a description of the differences between *sacred sites* and *power places*.

SACRED SITES

Sacred sites are places of religious or historical importance for aboriginal people. A sacred site can also be a spot or location where a sacred person has visited, lived, performed miracles, said prayers upon or become enlightened. For instance, the Bodhi Tree where Buddha meditated and became enlightened was already a holy place. Buddha's enlightenment at that spot gave it another dimension of sacredness.

The appearance of the Blessed Virgin Mary at a cave in Lourdes France is another example of a place that was already considered holy (the cave) being visited by a sacred person (Blessed Virgin Mary). The eighteen visions of Bernadeta Sobirós (now, Saint Bernadette), further evidenced the sacredness of the site.

Other sacred places upon the landscape may have forever been regarded as holy, showing evidence of continuous occupation or reverence from the earliest of times. The Chartres Cathedral in France was previously a well that was a pilgrimage site; and, before that, a Druid site. Civilizations continued to build sacred places atop those of the past.

It is often believed that sacred sites are the homes of gods or sacred beings. Divination is often practiced at sacred sites, based on the idea that the gods or other powerful supernatural forces can reveal information and knowledge about the present and future. The Oracle at Delphi in Greece is an example of a sacred site specifically known for divination.

The ancient Greeks sited a shrine at Delphi to honor the earth Goddess Gaia. Their choice of location was not by chance...The sages asserted among other things that a mysterious substance called the "plenum" bubbled up from the ground there in abundance and that such an abundance favored Gaia and the work of the priestess oracle, Pithia, to prophesy... Modern psychology and design have tossed aside such ideas of places of power, but our bodies and minds still hear their call and respond to them.
James A. Swan, *The Power of Place and Human Environments*

POWER PLACES

Spiritual explorers (also called pilgrims) make power places their destinations, often inspired by the sacred ambience or a mystical, magical energy. They feel a particular relationship to a place or make a journey based on a calling they receive to visit.

Many original natural features and power places have been altered by man; like building a church over a sacred stone or rock. In these instances the power place becomes inseparable from the structure built at the place.

> *Grace Cathedral (in San Francisco) is sited on an ancient*
> *Indian sacred place marked by two artesian springs.*
> James A. Swan, *The Power of Place & Human Environments*

The Cathedral of Santo Domingo in Cuzco, Peru is an example of such a place. Beneath the Christian structure is Kiswarkancha (today known as Qoricancha), the Inca palace of Viracocha, ruler of Cuzco. The Temple of the Sun stood as the center or navel of the world and remnants of it can be seen today inside the existing structure.

Every power place owes its significance to its geomantic location and may also be consecrated by human or divine activity. Geomancy is divination of the landscape—the knowledge of the relationship between topography, watercourses, natural qi and human alteration of the landscape. Following are some identifiers of power places:

- where sky meets earth on top of a mountain or hill

- earth, sky and water conjunct

- a major river rises from the earth

- where fire and water mix—a hot spring

- a cave

- a mountain pass

- confluences of ley lines

Besides auspicious geomantic features, great rocks (mountains, particular peaks), lakes and springs, confluences of water and sky, and burial sites are often power places.

Where Are Sacred Places?

Her citizens, imperial spirits, rule the present from the past.
Percy Bysshe Shelly, *Hellas*

We have established, built, named and visited sacred places in every corner of the world since our arrival on the planet. During our distant past we were connected to nature—earth, sky and the elements. As natural seers—knowledge was intuitive, communication was telepathic and energy could be seen and sensed. Places of exceptional earth energy were recognized, and we knew these places acted as gateways to higher realms. We instinctively knew the soul was nurtured and uplifted by visiting sacred places.

Today, sacred places continue to send their magnetic vibrations across the planet, inviting us to visit. Books, magazines and visual media, rich with images and stories of places of antiquity and long lost civilizations, inspire us and stir our curiosity. The Great Pyramid at Giza and The Sphinx in Egypt; Delphi, Greece, where the oracle spoke to sovereigns; the majestic mountaintop city of Machu Picchu in Peru; megalithic stone circles like Stonehenge and the Mayan pyramids of Central America—are a few examples.

Now, as in ancient times, sacred places are powerful, vibrant transmitters and receptive beneficiaries of experience and wisdom. Records of the past and visions of the future reveal themselves intimately and personally to visitors who are open and sensitive to their messages.

At sacred places the veils between the worlds are thin,
even transparent. Those who normally do not see the people, places
and things inhabiting invisible worlds, have visions and revelatory dreams.

Examples of some of the best known sacred places are listed below. This is a random list and in no way indicates these particular places have greater power or significance than any of the thousand's of sacred places around the world:

AUSTRALIA	Uluru
CAMBODIA	Angkor Wat
EGYPT	Great Pyramid & Sphinx
ENGLAND	Stonehenge
GREECE	Delphi
GUATEMALA	Tikal, Lake Atitlan, Quirigua
INDIA	Mahabodhi Temple, Kashi Vishwanath Temple, Varanasi
ITALY	St. Peter's Basilica, Rome
MEXICO	Chichen Itza, Palenque
PERU	Machu Picchu
SAUDI ARABIA	Kaaba, Mecca
TIBET	Lhasa, Mt. Kailash
TOYKO	Meiji Shrine
TURKEY	Hagia Sofia
UNITED STATES	Sedona, Cahokia Mounds, Chaco Canyon

PLACEMENT AND LOCATION

Every physical influence, including the frequency and vibration of the earth, designated the placement and location of sacred places. The design of the structure or site was intended to enhance the consciousness and energy levels of visitors. The sun, the moon and the stars dictated specific locations to capture the energy according to the seasons.

The King's chamber in the great pyramid at Giza, Glastonbury Tor in England and Sinagua and Anasazi sites in the Southwest, USA, are aligned with the constellation of Orion.

An example of a specific alignment can be seen at the temple Chichen Itza, in Yucatan, Mexico, where Kukulkan, the feathered serpent of Mayan lore, ascends the pyramid steps at the fall equinox and descends them in the spring—all through the movement of light. Tiahuanaco in Bolivia is aligned with the Winter Solstice. Stonehenge,

England, is aligned with the summer solstice sunrise. Solstice and equinox times are ideal for sacred rituals as the energy is strongest and can be directed toward connecting with higher realms, healing or fertility.

The most powerful sacred places are those where you connect deeply and receive the most value.

Many Types of Sacred Places

Sacred places exist worldwide and in many forms. While ancient places are not all sacred, each place has a story to tell. Below are some examples of the different types of sacred places:

NATURAL SITES

Mountains, caves, unique natural features on the earth, forests, trees, groves, landscape carvings: *Mt. Kailash, Tibet; Mt. Shasta, USA; San Francisco Peaks, Flagstaff, Arizona USA.*

SACRED WATERS

Wells, springs, cenotes, rivers, lakes: *Chalice Well, England; Montezuma's Well, Arizona, USA.*

HOLY PLACES

Shrines, altars, places where relics are kept, birth and death places of saints, apparition sites, Marian sites, monasteries, tombs of saints, sanctuaries, places where miracles have occurred, places where enlightenment has occurred, miracle working statues or icons: *Potala Palace, Lhasa, Tibet; Our Lady of Guadalupe, Mexico.*

STRUCTURES

Temples and cathedrals, pyramids, ruins: *Luxor Temple, Egypt; Tikal, Guatemala; Templa; Copan, Honduras.*

EARTHWORKS

Labyrinths, medicine wheels, megalithic-chambered mounds and earth mounds, standing stones, landscape carvings: *Big Horn Medicine Wheel, USA; Cahokia Mounds, Illinois USA; Carnac, France; Newgrange, Ireland.*

UNIQUE LOCATIONS

Creation story locations and boundaries, burial sites, sacred portals recounting star migration (past and present), places of prehistoric revelation, spirit sites, locations of mythological importance, ceremonial sites, places chosen by animals or birds, astronomical observatories, stones of healing and power, oracular sites, places of attained enlightenment, places of emergence, dragon sightings and slayings. Sacred islands and places chosen by divinatory methods like dowsing: *Mahabodhi Temple, Doorway of Amaru Meru, Lake Titicaca, Peru; Delphi, Greece; Monte Alban, Mexico.*

Why Do We Visit Sacred Places?

There is a record of sacred places written on our soul and incised on our bones—a song, imprinted on our DNA and flowing through us like the blood that feeds our body.

To visit a sacred place is a calling—a desire to renew a connection or feel there is something a particular place has to impart to us. We are not alone in these inclinations—we have been anointed with the elixir of deep soul memory, demanding our presence at locations near and far. Many of us will travel to sacred places to restore our multidimensional self to wholeness—to surrender the limited self and reconnect with the Eternal Divine Self.

Our multi-sensory system is tuned to specific vibrations and frequencies. We contact and connect with those beings and events present on our frequency and timeline.

On a multidimensional clock or calendar, our arrival has been awaited, and we are honored guests carrying valuable information and insights in our energy fields. Visiting sacred places broadens our perspective and rearranges our priorities. We see ourselves more clearly, helping us to define our purpose.

Sacred places trigger memories of our Eternal Divine Self, bring clarity and reveal our next steps.

These mysterious ancient places awaken, inspire, heal, catalyze and gracefully instill the qualities of wisdom, compassion, peace of mind and insight in those who visit. Many cannot describe their reasons for wanting to visit a sacred place. Afterwards, it may be difficult to describe exactly what happened. Inevitably, a great shift or change takes place—one that is often beyond words.

The magic of sacred places is reflected in myths and
legends that speak of healing, enlightenment,
increased creativity, amplified psychic abilities, clarity and
a heightened sense of self and purpose.

Benefits of the Journey
The most beautiful thing we can experience is the mysterious.
It is the source of all true art and all science. He to whom this emotion is
a stranger, who can no longer pause to wonder and stand rapt in awe,
is as good as dead: his eyes are closed.
Albert Einstein

The journey you choose to make to a sacred place may challenge you spiritually, physically, emotionally and psychologically. This is all part of the matrix of change. Why make such a journey? What are the potential benefits one might expect to receive from visiting a sacred place? Identify any expectations for the changes that might transpire. Become aware of any intentions you may have for the journey.

When we visit sacred sites we go there with humility,
perform our acts of respect and then see what happens—
we surrender to the place rather than try to 'control' it.
James Swan. *Sacred Places,*
How the Living Earth Seeks our Friendship

Here are a few of the potential benefits:

• Receiving a vision illuminating a course or mission to pursue.

• Gives life new significance.

- Completing a journey to a sacred place instills confidence in one's abilities and strength.

- Real or imagined limitations are transcended when you survive the journey.

- Discover additional sources of power beyond yourself.

- Enhance your link to humanity.

- Receive inner revelations and profound meaning for the direction of your life.

- Develop a deeper connection with yourself, the natural world, society and the soul.

- A deep connection with nature promotes understanding of yourself as an organic part of the process.

- Deep realization that nature is our home…breathtakingly beautiful, nurturing and vibrantly alive.

- Learn to allow your Eternal Divine Self to take the lead and inform decisions.

- Develop a stronger appreciation for your friends and relations

- Develop a stronger appreciation for life and material comforts.

- Release illusions.

- Learn to rely upon yourself as your own source of wisdom rather than looking outward for answers (teachers, books, churches, gurus).

- Establish a deeper connection to the mystical and mythological aspects of life.

- Receive a new direction, foundation in life, self-definition and values.

- Become familiar with the ancestors, spirits and guardians present in other dimensions.

- Receive answers to life's questions.

- Awaken to the truth.

Our finely tuned sensitivity and awareness is an accurate indicator of all changes—subtle or easily observable—physical, emotional, mental and spiritual.

Tourism and Sacred Places

Tourists don't know where they've been;
travelers don't know where they're going.
Paul Theroux

Tourism is the economic backbone of many countries and cities around the world. In most instances, tour providers—both traditional and spiritual—are focused on the skillful management of people in and out of a variety of conveyances and locations according to a timetable to fulfill a schedule. The nature of tourism is to have the visitor *see* as much as possible of a country or place during their visit. During this *sightseeing*, photos are taken, many words are spoken, and the tourist can say, "Yes, I have been there."

What about the spiritual explorer who makes a journey based upon a calling and desires a deep connection with sacred places?

The spiritual explorer is seeking something tourism
does not address—that which is hidden and invisible.
It takes an easy, relaxed, multi-sensory interaction with
sacred places to access what lies in invisible realms.

Often, long distances are traveled at great expense and the last thing we want to experience is being flashed through a site at lightning speed with a guide parroting stories and pointing out what is important for us to see.

Spiritual Archaeologists mine the spiritual wealth of sacred places.

The material in this book will initiate the spiritual explorer into the practice of Spiritual Archaeology and Practical Shamanism used at sacred places. You do not have to travel to distant lands to implement this knowledge—yet, should you have such a journey in mind, this book will be perfect companion material.

When to Visit Sacred Places

Traditional religious people often visit the sites tied to the history of their religion. Pilgrimages (i.e., *Santiago de Compostela*) may happen all at once or over a number of years. Buddhists may choose to visit the places that Buddha is known to have visited. Christians may be attracted to the places of miracles, like Lourdes in France; Jews, The Temple Mount and Muslims visit Mecca. Other religious groups may seek out those sites of historical and religious significance to them— temples, cathedrals, and shrines.

Many sacred places have been set up to highlight Equinox and Solstice times. Dates of festivals, ceremonies, religious holidays and celebrations are also popular travel times. Spiritual explorers appear to have an internal clock indicating when it is time to visit. Inner knowing often catalyzes our journeys. We may hear *the call*.

THE CALL

Being sensitive to when we are *called* to a site is an excellent way to decide when to go. Often, there is some attraction to an area; we read something, know of a specific journey, are drawn to images in magazines and movies, or the mention of a place keeps appearing in conversation. We can choose to pay attention to these signals, or not.

We may have an awareness of a past life, historical connection, wisdom teaching, or strong interest drawing us to visit a sacred place. There are times we just go and find out later what the draw was all about. Use the following exercise as a way to determine whether a place and time is right for you:

- Use the Spiritual Energy Expansion Nucleus (SEEN) outlined in the next section of this book to relax, center and focus inward.

- Concentrate on an image of the destination you have in mind.

- With the image in place, see the proposed date of travel printed on the lower edge the image.

- Imagine yourself in the picture, walking, sitting, exploring.

- Notice how you feel and how your body responds to being in the location of your inquiry.

- Ask if the guardians and the sacred place(s) are ready to receive you at this time.

- Tune into and scan you body for signals and feelings.

- If a feeling is less than positive and uplifting, follow through by asking what the feeling is about.

- Come to completion with your process of looking inward.

- Write down what you have discovered.

If you think you will not hear the call or recognize the right time to travel, simply choose a place and time that appeals to you and go. One thing leads to another, and you will find yourself off on the journey of a lifetime.

CHOOSE YOUR TIME

Choices about times of day and season to visit a sacred place can be based on comfort and quiet. Whenever possible, avoid fighting the elements (cold, rain, intense heat) and the crowds. In a hotter climate, choose very early morning or late afternoon—in cooler climates, choose afternoons when the sun is at its zenith, providing maximum warmth.

Do you really want to be at a sacred place with thousands of people? Maybe you do! Possibly there will be no choice in the matter. Consider your personality and how you might best enjoy your time at sacred places.

Seek the most peaceful and quiet moments when the fewest number of people are around and the crowds have left or not yet arrived. Locate a quiet, less visited area of the site. Undisturbed, you can connect with nature and the earth; enjoy the subtle sounds of animals and birds, the wind in the trees.

What Happens at Sacred Places?

Swirling smoky trails of incense and sounds of chanting and drumming
may have filled the air for hundreds or thousands of years before
our arrival. We become part of an ongoing ceremony as our feet
touch the earth and we walk through sacred places.

Sacred places hold many keys to the nature, cycle and unfolding of our lives. When we visit sacred places, we are able to sense in new and different ways, and we know on a very deep level that something has shifted or clarified within us. While we may not be able to measure what happens in a scientific way, we sense that hidden dimensions beyond our range of normal sight are operating.

Since all matter is condensed light, light is the source,
the cause of life. Therefore, light is divine. The flowers have
a direct line to God that an evangelist would kill for.
Tom Robbins

We enter into the energy field of a site when we arrive in the immediate area. The energy field of a sacred place is teeming with information that saturates the natural elements (earth, stones, waters, trees, plants) and structures at the location. As we walk through a site in the third dimension, we pass by and through mystical doorways reaching far into the past and future. Our energy field connects with the fields of the site, exchanging and sharing information and possibilities in much the same way we do when we meet with a friend, associate, mentor or lover.

Each conscious footstep we take at a sacred place is a merging of spirit;
human, trees, rocks, air, animals, ancestors, wind, sky, water,
the beings of the earth upon which we walk.
A nonstop stream of information flows to us and through us
as the information we carry is shared in return.

A transference of energy takes place between sacred places and the visitor. As visitors to these sites, we record our impressions with video, photography or audio devices. We point a camera in the direction of a specific doorway or rock formation, hoping to capture something that can be felt rather than seen. Simultaneously, the earth records impressions of our visits, our energy, and the record of our soul remains in the energy field of the site.

Our presence at sacred places is recorded and
becomes part of the energy field of that place.

Phenomena occurring at sacred places are produced by the cumulative experience of all who have visited and the events that have occurred—all retained in the energy field of the site itself.

Sacred places and specific locations within the site
are encircled by distinct and information-rich fields of energy.

The specific placement or location of sacred places allows for a steady stream of life force to emanate from them. Celestial and earthly alignments are calculated to enhance our lives, charge our energy, heal and revitalize our bodies. Ongoing visits and intentions for sacred places keep them alive.

The scalp prickles when we pass a certain ancient doorway;
we shiver, spine-chilled, in such a spot as the ceremonial cavern
at Bandelier; the voice drops to a whisper at Chartres...
D.M. Dooling. "Focus," *Parabola* 3 issue 1, 1978

The influence of the stars beaming spiritual energy onto the earth, the matrix of ley lines (read: *Ley Lines and Earth Energies*, David Cowan and Chris Arnold) crisscrossing the planet and connecting sacred places and myths and legends telling of the alchemy of times past, all leave their indelible imprint.

We are catalyzed onward in our life's journey; we gain greater clarity and make better decisions; we release the past and make way for the new; we see ourselves and the world in a different way. This invisible yet palpable power refreshes and stabilizes us.

Everything is significant when we are at a sacred place. The presence of an animal brings messages and teachings to us. The flight of eagle may remind us to choose a higher perspective, since the eagle flies higher than any other bird. The snake that sheds its skin by crawling out of it may appear to remind us that we are in a cycle of transformation, shedding the old (skin).

We may not understand the song the bird sings,
but we can be certain that the vibration
of its song feeds into our field and
is sent as a loving and healing gift.

Stones, mountains, waters or whatever a site holds also send out a song (vibration), although silent in most cases.

We meet ourselves on a deeper level at sacred places.
Much as a student can learn from a meeting with a great master,
we access greater wisdom within ourselves during these journeys.

When we are at the site, engrossed in the moment, it is not always possible to decipher the messages we are receiving. Signals and vibrations broadcasting into our energy field often wait for translation later. We receive messages that are uniquely ours. There is no right way to receive a message or to interpret it. You are the master interpreter.

INVISIBLE WORLDS
Perceiving, accessing and interacting with all
levels of creation is our human destiny.

Through our eyes we see only 5% of the world around us, unaware of the matrix connecting all life; blind to the multidimensional worlds and beings that surround us. *We are multidimensional beings living in a multidimensional universe—spirit in the material world, in a physical body.*

When we choose to allow our full perceptive abilities to operate,
we gain access to multidimensional reality, the realm of spirit, and
cumulative knowledge of those who came before.

Levels of life beyond linear time, eclipsed from our ordinary vision, are the domain of shamans, seers, mystics and medicine people who regularly commune with the world of spirit and delve into the unseen and invisible. They perceive all matter as alive, as living energy. Sacred places are vibrantly alive and one of the living realms of spirit.

Silence is a powerful practice supporting our dialogue
and connection with the unseen.

People in cultures around the world honor their ancestors; altars are kept and offerings are made to those who live in other dimensions. Multidimensional reality is integrated as part of life, and the beings that inhabit it are known and honored. Indigenous cultures recognize the gods or the sacred energy of rivers, stones, mountains, earth, streams, animals and all elements of nature.

The fact that we have been disconnected from
the natural world and rhythms of the universe for so long
does not foretell a permanent condition.

We are conditioned to perceive the world in a linear manner and to use our five senses and logical mind as the main information sources. What is known as extrasensory perception is rapidly becoming the new *normal*.

Interactions with sacred places involve a willingness
to enter into the realm of spirit; our innate
multi-sensory system connects us with invisible worlds.

THE INFLUENCE OF MYTHOLOGY

Obscured by the veils of time, myths have been erroneously mislaid in the realm of fable, invention, fantasy or simple fiction. Ancient myths echo from times long gone, are translated from languages since forgotten and speak of worlds that have become invisible. The beings, places and events inhabiting these old stories seem unbelievable to us in modern times. Myths hale from beyond this world, at the time of beginnings and speak of mystical or supernatural experience. As fantastic as it may seem, myths simply state what happened.

The heroes and superhuman beings we meet in myths display their sacred powers to model behaviors, morals and the meanings of life for us. We interpret what we cannot understand, personally experience, or see as the actions of supernatural, superhuman beings as the acts of gods.

These gods were often tied to sacred places (i.e. *Cave of Zeus* in Greece). King Arthur of the Round Table and his knights (Glastonbury, England); Arjuna and Krishna of the *Bhagavad-Gita* (Cave of Arjuna); the Homeric epics (Crete, Greek island of the Gods); and the Sumerian *Gilgamesh* (Garden of the gods) are a few examples of great and enduring stories. These stories give us insights into different cultures, times, traditions and outlooks, expanding our view of the world, possibilities and ourselves.

Creation myths appear in every culture, outlining stories of emergence and beginnings of the creator gods. The *Rig Veda* of India, the Egyptian *Atum* and the Hebrew *Genesis* are examples of creation myths.

Myths and legends are passed down through oral traditions, from generation to generation, providing answers to the basic questions of life: *Who am I? Why am I here? What is my purpose? What is my role? How do I fit into the human and natural world? How should I live?* A myth can assist us on our walk through life, giving us a sense of what our journey is about and how others have prevailed against similar challenges.

Our human journey is translated into cosmological terms through myths. Every myth and legend contains some truth and when our hearts open, we see and hear the story beneath the myth and feel it is spoken directly to us, about us, and for us.

It is always wise to reap the benefits of the lessons from those who have already walked the paths we find ourselves upon. Spiritual Archaeologists often consider myths in their explorations, seeing clearly and personally what value a myth may hold. A great story, like a great piece of art, allows the viewer total freedom of interpretation. In this way, each person can see their own story revealed, their beliefs out-pictured, and their challenges made clear.

We play a variety of roles at different times in our lives, and so our role within a myth will change as well. We may embody or embrace the characteristics of Athena and go on to integrate Venus or Isis. It is not as if one myth will guide us for a lifetime. If we are committed to change, we are likely to pass through many characters and stories, each holding a piece of the great mystery and the saga of our lives.

In the distant past, the gods made their presence known and were not strictly consigned to heaven or some invisible place—they were seen and heard. Animals, people, stones, mountains, rivers, streams, buildings and even time itself was held as sacred and each one had a voice.

Sacred places located around the world are dignified as *sacred* due to events that have taken place in the past—and continue to take place today. The reason supernatural and paranormal aspects of sacred places have continued to attract visitors is partially due to myths and legends, large and small, continuously recited up to this day. They are passed from people who visit the sites, to other people who may not yet done so. We are the modern-day makers and performers in the new myths and legends.

EXPECT THE UNEXPECTED

If the doors of perception were cleansed,
everything would appear to man as it is, infinite.
William Blake

Journeys to sacred places provide an opportunity to step into dimensions and realities that differ from what we are accustomed to in our everyday life. It is important to be sensitive to ourselves, others and the delicate environments we explore. The more sensitivity we can practice, the richer our experience will be.

Drop any expectations–leave them behind. Taking the time to be informed has great value, and you may find all you have read, heard or thought about a sacred place is about to be shown as inadequate or simply wrong.

When we are truly open and sensitive, our experience is unlikely
to match our expectations. The unexpected meeting, situation, realization
or vision is a teller of truths. Be observant and receptive.

TIMELESSNESS

We step into multidimensional reality at sacred places—a realm where time does not exist. Ideas of good, bad, right or wrong are also nonexistent. Here, we expertly reach through the veils of illusion and vastness of experience and wisdom to find the exact information, remedies, balms, answers, and visions for the ever-present Eternal Now.

WHAT YOU SEE IS WHAT YOU GET

There is no fixed reality here.

It was late afternoon on an overcast August day and I was the guide for three spiritual explorers in Sedona, Arizona. We were driving down a dirt road going toward a place in the desert for a fire ceremony.

A woman in the back seat called out, "Look, a cat." I stopped the car and from the left side came a wild cat who crossed in front of the car and bounded up the embankment on the right and on into the desert. It happened in an instant and I was amazed at what I saw. Living here for over twenty years, I had never seen a wild cat.

It was a couple days later while talking to a friend when it occurred to me that we might have, as people often do—seen different things. I emailed the other people who were in the car asking them to tell me what they saw.

The woman who spotted the cat and called out to us saw a "tan or light brown colored fur, no markings. The cat weighed about thirty pounds."

Another woman saw "a thickly furred, medium sized feline with a graceful power to its stride and a curious gaze. Its fur was dappled with dark spots and bands, while the majority of it was the color of sand, only with more of a caramel tone to it. The tail was a black stub and it seemed to have pointed ears with long fur rising from them. It looked to weigh about fifty pounds."

The man saw "a large tan cat weighing in at around a hundred pounds."

I saw a cat of approximately 4-5 feet in length from head to tail that weighed at least 80 pounds, maybe more. The cat was bright golden orange with black spots, rosettes, and stripes at the hindquarter. For me, it had an electric brilliance to the colors—it appeared to be a jaguar.

Whatever you see and experience is meant specifically for you and is to be trusted completely. It may not be what others see, even if they are standing right next to you. Two people standing in the same place at the same time, looking at the same thing, see and experience differently. This is one way we recognize the distortions of history, *his story*. *His story* is only one viewpoint, not necessarily the one we may want to embrace as truth.

As Spiritual Archaeologists, we rely upon and trust
our own insights and information—fully.

There is no right or wrong, better or worse, good or bad, there is simply what *is* for each of us. Our perception defines our reality experience. Trusting what we see gives each of us accurate information.

AM I HEARING THINGS?

Our clairaudient abilities come alive at sacred places. It is not unusual to hear a word shouted out, or a name, or other information. Directions like "stop," "go left," "sit down" are more easily heard at sacred places. Words or phrases may come into your head—just listen. Don't judge it, just listen and be willing to open to more information. Always trust the information you receive.

AM I SEEING THINGS?

Did the rocks suddenly show me a picture of something or someone? Did I imagine that rock just became transparent and I could see inside? Did someone walk into the shadows in back of that temple? Our abilities to see the invisible world become greatly enhanced at sacred places. Take note, pay attention and allow the images or visions to emerge.

THOUGHTS ARE CLUES

Notice you thoughts and follow them through. Does the thought you are thinking have anything to do with the place you are standing, the event that just occurred or words that were just spoken?

SEE THE OTHER SIDE

If you have always thought things were one way, you may find reversals on your journey. Discoveries we make as Spiritual Archaeologists often present a whole new side of life. Be willing to accept that things may be very different from how you previously perceived them.

Self As Sacred Place

The study of mysteries requires a courage and a willingness
to participate in a powerful adventure of the soul
that is at once both universal and intensely personal.
Jean Houston

Our travels to sacred places are a lens through which we view, examine and come to know more about the sacred place closest to home—our Self. As spirits in the material world, we inhabit a physical body, a temple and sanctuary supporting the indwelling sacredness of life itself. Each of us has written on our soul the wisdom of all times, the magic and miracles dreamed and performed and the absolute heights to which humanity has aspired and achieved during our long earthly walk.

As sacred and divine beings we have the inherent abilities to know, change, heal and transform anything. Choosing to live life in the natural flow of the universe is one key to experiencing the magic of life itself.

I am a trusting leaf being carried along
on the stream of life.

Places of peaceful refuge, (i.e. a garden, a special walk or a meditation space) restore, replenish and renew us for the journey through life. Visiting sacred places located away from home shifts the matrix of day-to-day life initiating a revitalizing effect as multidimensional aspects of our being are revealed. Can we sit in a sacred space at home and simultaneously visit a sacred site? Yes, absolutely!

We have within us everything necessary
to project our consciousness anywhere
in this world or beyond.

Each of us is a sacred place to be honored, respected, revered and loved. Our journey through this life and the experiences we create leads us to the Eternal Divine Self, who we really are. We are sacred places, each of us—godlike beings.

As we reclaim the Eternal Divine Self,
we initiate and sustain the highly desirable effect of
overriding the limitations present in consensus reality.

II.
SEEN

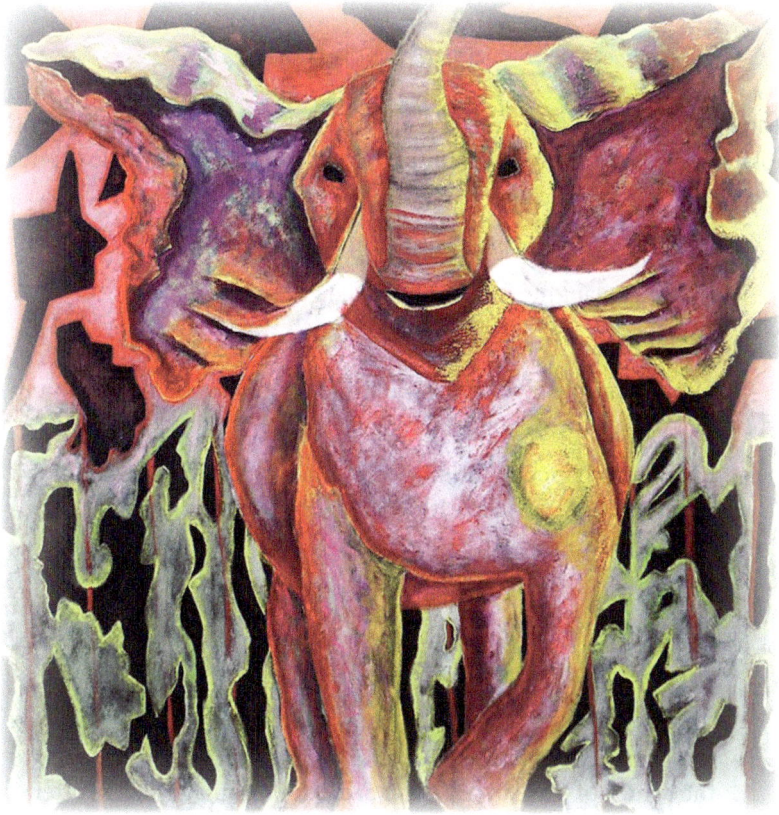

SEEN

To see and be seen.

Spiritual Energy Expansion Nucleus – SEEN

SEEN is a three step process preparing us to connect with the information and beings at sacred places in the invisible realms of existence. The invisible can be *seen* and so can we. The SEEN process will appear in exercises throughout the book and can be used for any type of divining activity. The SEEN process fosters a strong and stable energy system for the Spiritual Archaeologist.

STEP 1: GROUND

When we ground ourselves, we bring all our aspects into present time—Now, and stabilize the physical body. Any excess energy accumulated during sessions or interactions with other beings or dimensions will naturally flow into the earth. Eliminate all distractions and noises—TV's, radios and computers. Enter into silence and close your eyes.

- Keep the spine erect so energy can flow freely.

- If sitting, plant the feet firmly on the ground,

- If lying, place the hands and arms at your sides.

- Exhale completely. All the old, tired energy leaves the body and makes way for the new.

- Inhale will happen automatically, filling your chest to abdomen area with new, fresh breath. Feel the revitalizing energy entering the body with the breath.

- Invite all aspects of your multidimensional self to be fully present with you.

- Use a series of eight breaths in this way to feel grounded and centered. Do eight more breaths as needed.

- See a golden cord of light extend from the base of your spine to the center of the earth. (This cord can be dematerialized after your session or interaction is complete.)

- Scan the body for any areas of tension, stress, pain, holding or tightness.

- Breathe into the area of discomfort and as you exhale, release the energy down to the center of the earth where it can be used as fuel or nutrients.

- Enjoy feeling grounded and present.

STEP 2: EXPAND THE ENERGY FIELD
A field of energy surrounds the physical body and contracts and expands with feelings, situations, health, environments and relationships. We can consciously expand the energy field, making it as large as we want. When our field is larger we feel alive, present, centered and confident—we can vibrate our light and essence fully.

- After grounding, continue to exhale fully and allow the breath to automatically fill your body.

- With each inhale, imagine the energy field surrounding you body getting larger while simultaneously being filled with light.

- Choose the colors of the rainbow or any single color to fill the field with light.

- Feel the light surrounding you and warming you.

- Expand the energy field a minimum of six feet from your body.

- Circulate the light and energy in your field. Flowing and moving the light within the energy field continually refreshes and restores the physical and mental body while boosting psychic abilities.

- Imagine a waterfall effect where the color of light you have chosen flows downward, upward, or in a circular direction around the body. This vibrant flowing energy field automatically releases anything you no longer need to hold or carry and repels any type of negativity or infringement.

- Relax into the feeling of presence and energy expansion.

STEP 3: HEART-OPENING BREATH

One way to shift to inner knowing is to move our consciousness from the head to the heart—operate from a feeling center rather than left-brain logic. A heart centered reality naturally aligns with the universe and planet. Heart centered awareness illuminates the core and nature of people, places and events. You will recognize what harmonizes with you and what does not.

The Heart-Opening Breath is a centering, grounding and meditative breath as useful in everyday life as it is on journeys to sacred places. The breath clears the mind of chatter, psychological assessment and other distractions and opens the heart. Use this breath any time throughout the day when you want to relax, refocus or come back to center.

- Lying, standing and sitting are all perfect positions for this practice.

- Close the eyes.

- Place both hands over the heart—the center of the chest.

- Breath naturally for a minute.

- Feel your chest rising and falling as you inhale and exhale.

- Inhale. Draw your breath in through the top of your head—the crown chakra.

- See this breath as a beam of cleansing and revitalizing light.

- Choose a color for the light.

- Feel the light sweeping all thoughts away, cleansing the mind.

- See and feel any mental clutter transformed into golden stardust.

- Feel the golden stardust cascade from your mind to your heart, nurturing and revitalizing the heart.

- Exhale…breathing out through your heart.

- Focus on your heart as your chest rises and falls with each breath.

- Breathe in through the crown and out through the heart.

- Continue breathing this way focusing on the heart.

- Feel the warmth, peace and calm when consciousness is heart centered.

- Become aware of heightened sensitivity as you relax deeply.

- Remove the hands from the chest once the breath is stabilized.

- As you exhale through the heart, stream the vibration of love out into the world.

SEEN produces a state of relaxation and heightened sensitivity, supporting communication with all beings: animals, plants, rocks, waters and whatever exists in this or other dimensions. It sets up a frequency and vibration allowing us to commune with invisible worlds.

III.
SPIRITUAL
ARCHAEOLOGY

SPIRITUAL ARCHAEOLOGY

Spiritual Archaeology is a multi-sensory search and exploration
of the unseen realms of existence to discover hidden origins, practices,
customs, stories and deeper meanings beyond the material
evidence of ancient civilizations and cultures.
Personal, historical and spiritual meanings emerge.

Archaeological excavators do not recognize spiritual energies or the wealth of information present in unseen realms. Spiritual Archaeology explorations present us with remembrances, stories, feelings, and visions that are most relevant to our personal myths and our unique, individual, evolutionary process. "His" story (history) is not our story and while they are all stories, more value can be derived from our unique personal discoveries.

The old paradigm of being led around like sheep and adapting to obsolete
cultural models and outdated conditioning has ended.

Spiritual Archaeologists come from every educational background, religion, belief system, nationality and age group. They instinctively know the timeless wisdom traditions of the ancients reflect the highest potential of the human spirit for internal peace, happiness and the inspired expression of spirit in the material world. Practitioners of Spiritual Archaeology know that the past is not behind us, the future is not ahead, and that we are living in the ever-present Now.

As Spiritual Archaeologists we examine, decipher and translate
information based on our individual understandings and beliefs.
Our interpretations may not match those of others,
and that is as it should be.

How did our ancestors answer humanity's fundamental questions? *Is this all there is? Why am I here, and what is my purpose? Is there something greater in the universe that compels me? What happens after death? Have I been here before? What is the most important thing for me to know right now?*

We are destined to find our own answers, live fearlessly in the truth
of who we are, and take a bit of wisdom from those who came before.

A Spiritual Archaeologist may choose to look into specific people, events or civilizations and access subtleties, thoughts, beliefs and practices. Individual discoveries might include one's role in the community, relationships, ritualistic practices, etc. Cosmic principles and learning can be acquired, leading to well being. It is not unusual to receive information that contradicts the mainstream viewpoints of historians and traditional archaeologists.

Spiritual Archaeology Principles

One's destination is never a place, but a new way of seeing things.
Henry Miller

As Spiritual Archaeologists, we model new behaviors and ways of visiting and interacting with sacred places and the people of the lands on which they rest. Below are basic principles to follow:

- **Environment:** Learn about environmental sustainability and natural habitats and become familiar with the delicate environments to be visited.

- **Impact:** Spiritual Archaeology takes us to natural, fragile, pristine and protected areas including tribal lands, archaeological sites and cultural heritage sites. Our visits to these areas are done on a small scale (small numbers of people—or larger groups split into smaller groups) to reduce effects on delicate environments.

- **Indigenous Customs:** Honor the local customs, traditions, beliefs and intentions for the site—be sensitive and respectful. Honor differences. Indigenous people are often the caretakers and stewards of sacred places. If you don't know, ask.

- **Inclusion:** Acquire permission to enter specific areas or locations. Welcome the participation of the local people and invite them to lecture and speak or guide. Invite local shamans, medicine people and elders to perform ceremonies and share stories and traditions.

- **Respect:** Do not override or overlay traditions, ceremonies, rituals and customs practiced and maintained by local people.

- **Pay it Forward—physical:** We receive wonderful, life changing gifts from the locations and cultures we visit. Find ways to provide direct financial benefits for conservation and/or to benefit local people or causes in the locations visited.

- **Pay it Forward—spiritual:** When we ask for or seek something from sacred places, it is customary to return a gift. All interactions with sacred places, guardians of sites (invisible) and any inter-dimensional beings are sacred. Your gift can be a prayer of gratitude and blessing.

- **Representation:** Be impeccable with what you do and say. Our actions inform the behaviors of others.

- **Assumptions:** Assume nothing, always ask. For example, taking photos of tribal or indigenous people is not always an acceptable practice. In some cultures, it is not allowed. In other places, people expect payment for allowing you to take a photo.

- **Site Etiquette:** Read Section VI of this book on outdoor and site etiquette.

General Preparation

Anticipation is part of the journey—a kind of pre-journey sparking our enthusiasm and inspiring us. The preparation we make in advance builds excitement and supports us to transition gracefully to our destination. Presented here are options you can choose to exercise. This is not a task list.

BEING INFORMED

If you enjoy research and reading, information gathering will be fun for you—bringing a rich awareness to the place(s) you plan to visit. Begin researching weeks or months before the actual journey. If you are not inclined to this type of pre-discovery, guiltlessly skip over this section. This is not a requirement—only a suggestion.

A psychological, emotional and psychic adjustment
will be taking place as we allow our imagination prior entry
to sacred places you plan to visit.

Informing ourselves by exploring the historical, anthropological, archaeological, cultural and spiritual dimensions of sacred places all contribute to our ability to link up with what is available to us personally. Each site holds invaluable treasures and our task is to be the open and willing recipients of those gifts.

Some of the resources available to explore prior findings and perspectives include books, movies, TV, academic journals, magazine articles, online resources, oral histories (audio), previous research and literature. Information derived from this exploration can trigger memories, visions, dreams or feelings. Embedded in the material are bits of inspiration supporting us to understand our particular relationship with sacred places. This is exactly what we are after. Categories you may consider pursuing include the following:

- **Science**—Ethnographic, biological, geological, ecological, geophysical, and paleontological data, among others, can be important to an understanding of the human past.

- **History**—comprises the events, patterns, and processes of the human past, including those that have affected literate societies and those that have affected preliterate or non-literate groups, whose history is sometimes known as prehistory.

- **Archaeology**—material remains (artifacts, structures, artworks, etc.) produced purposely or accidentally by human beings.

- **Material**—actual objects retrieved from a historic property as part of a data recovery program, including, but not limited to, artifacts, byproducts of human activity such as flakes of stone, fragments of bone, architectural materials and details, skeletal material, and works of art.

- **Myth and Legend**—stories grounded in truth provide strong reference points for what has transpired. The entire world and cultures within countries are rich in these stories, passed down in art, written and oral word. Unbelievable, in view of the world we inhabit today; yet beings (half beast and half human), giants, gods that flew through the sky and lived hundreds of years without aging–all existed and flourished. The worlds they created, built and lived in—what they believed, achieved and knew continues to be revealed.

Once you have learned all you have an appetite for, put away your materials. This journey is all about you. What you see, intuit, find, know, experience and come to understand about yourself, the site, and your connection to it is the gold to be mined.

RECORDING YOUR JOURNEY

Choose a recording device that is comfortable and easy for you to manage. Notebooks (paper or electronic), a camera (video or still) and voice recorders are excellent. Graphite or colored pencils are useful, if you like to draw.

Visual records remind us of time spent at a location, how it felt to be there, and other details we might easily forget. Photos sometimes-record things we do not see at the moment we snap the picture.

You may want to record the Spiritual Archaeology methods used to acquire information as well as any feelings or physical sensations you experienced at the site.

TIME CONSIDERATIONS

Plan to spend as much time as you desire at a location. Adequate time is needed for meditation, contemplation, writing or whatever suits your particular style of connecting.

CLIMATE–WEATHER–TERRAIN

Acquire a general description of the location you plan to visit including its size and terrain. Knowing the seasonal climate and prevailing weather is important. A rainy season, for instance, can be a muddy experience; often creating mudslides and other conditions prohibitive to travel.

Google Earth and GIS (geographic information systems) devices can be helpful and fun for explorations.

FIELD PROJECT RESEARCH DESIGN

A Field Project Research Design supports you to determine some of the things you would like to gain from the journey. Writing your research design in your notebook will formalize your intentions. Elements of this design might include:

- Indicating specific locations to explore at the site.

- Methods used to acquire information.

- Desired results of the exploration.

Research designs may be modified once on site, as the course of research yields new findings.

CREATE AND ANSWER RESEARCH QUESTIONS

Design a field project by asking questions about one or more locations at a specific site and decide what information you desire the location(s) to yield. The Spiritual Archaeologist is well served by approaching the site with a set of research questions in mind.

Research questions seek to identify locations, timeframes and activities at specific areas of a site. Questions can focus on acquiring information of a historical, personal, transformational or healing nature. Research questions are asked during a visit to a location. See the section on *Tools for the Spiritual Archaeologist* for ways to divine answers.

Examples of Questions:

- How was the site initially identified?

- What initially drew people to this site?

- When was the site or location first occupied?

- When was the site (or location at the site) last occupied?

- Were different parts of the site occupied simultaneously, or do they represent separate occupational episodes?

- What types of activities occurred at the site?

- How many people were in residence?

- Was there a difference in status between the people associated with the site?

- How were the different structures used?

- Do different areas of the site have different functions?

- Are there areas of the site with strong healing properties?

- Is there a specific location at the site I should focus upon? Where is it?

- What was the main accomplishment, use or contribution of the people here?

- Are there areas of the site associated with the lives of persons historically significant? Spiritually significant?

- Are there areas of the site where I should focus my research?

- Are there areas of the site associated with my past? Where are these areas? When was I here? What was my life about during that time? What parallels can I draw from that former life to this current one?

These are examples—add to or take away from the list. Your questions will help orient you to the site, focus your research and provide answers to your specific questions.

EXPLORING ARTIFACTS

Museums and visitor centers are repositories of artifacts collected from sacred places. Books and the internet have a wealth of images to imbibe. Take time to study or connect with these items before, during or after your visit to a site. Make notes and record your interpretations of the artifacts as a Spiritual Archaeologist. Can you sense the maker of an artifact, their thoughts, ideas and intentions?

AFTER YOUR VISIT

A vision turns to tiny particles and vanishes completely.

Impressions and insights often happen quickly and may have unusual qualities, imagery and content. Whenever possible, make a record immediately. Other dimensional experiences can be as elusive as a dream that fades quickly if we don't speak it or write it down. The notes and records you keep will be invaluable.

SHARING AND QUESTIONING

Whether you go alone or with friend, partner or a group, make time to discuss your findings. If you travel alone, talk to friends and associates about your experience when you return home. Others often have valuable insights that enhance or clarify a vision or understanding. We enrich each other by sharing.

MESSAGES COME SOONER—OR LATER

Sacred places share their information, wisdom and healing in different ways to each of us. Release any expectations around how information will come to you.

We may receive visions, messages, emotional clearings, insights and healing while at the site—or, notice that life has changed for the better after returning home. It is not always possible to put experience into words.

Tools for the Spiritual Archaeologist

Wakan Tanka, Great Mystery, teach me how to trust my heart,
my mind, my intuition, my inner knowing, the senses of my body,
the blessings of my spirit. Teach me to trust these things so that
I may enter my Sacred Space and love beyond my fear,
and thus Walk in balance with the passing of each glorious Sun.
Lakota Prayer

Sacred places are a living realm of spirit. Consistent acknowledgment of the presence of ancestors and spirits is openly practiced throughout the world in many cultures. Communication with the spirit world, multidimensional reality and sacred places is the practice of the Spiritual Archaeologist.

Spiritual Archaeologists develop finely tuned sensitivities,
use multi-sensory resources, focus inward and
communicate with the spirit world.

Traditional archaeology teaches us history through the collection, organization, and presentation of material culture finds. The archaeologist studies and interprets material objects that remain to understand a particular culture, their customs, rituals, and beliefs.

Spiritual Archaeology honors all information sources and
engages inner knowing and divining
to explore the invisible aspects of sacred places.

INNER KNOWING

A sense of direct contact with the ultimate reality has always been the realm of mystics and sages. Knowing that unity lies at the heart of the universe and seeing the interconnection of all life is at the core of our perceptive abilities.

The analytical left-brain is masterful at throwing objections in our path, blocking our natural intuition. Our conditioning—cultural, religious, educational, etc.—teaches us to listen to outside sources and authorities and rely upon what they have to sell or tell. It takes courage to step away from the norms society has established, regardless of how constricting they are.

Everyone from movie stars to New Age gurus are perceived as knowing something we do not. While each person you meet or observe in life carries messages of wisdom and enlightenment, they can only reflect or teach what you already know.

> *Our ability to remain unaffected by good or ill fortune*
> *is essential since neither has meaning in multidimensional reality.*

Have you ever read a book, watched a video or sat in a workshop only to think: *I knew that was going to happen.* When tuning into your bodily felt sense of a person or situation, you might have thought: *It feels right to me.* Developing trust happens over time. You may recognize how many times you knew the truth of a situation and ignored it.

> *We know who is on the phone before it rings,*
> *we think about an old friend and a letter arrives in the mail,*
> *the smell of a deceased grandfather's cigar*
> *wafts into the room when there is no one nearby.*

Teachers and guides are there to remind us of who we are and to open us to new ways of thinking and being. Placing anyone in a position of authority, relying upon answers they provide or being star struck in their presence is a distraction.

> *You are the only expert on your life, and your inner*
> *wisdom and truth are the gold you are on here to mine.*

Higher self, the *God presence within,* the *small still voice,* a *gut feeling* or *hunch* is our own inner knowing. *Intuition, insight* and *instinct* are all part of inner knowing. We are not taught or encouraged to honor our inner knowing, but to look for hard evidence from others.

Looking inward for answers and wisdom enables us to enter the realm of our Eternal Divine Self and access the unlimited power and wisdom of infinite domain. We can make a conscious upgrade in our operating system whenever we choose. Flip the switch.

We are told things have to be seen to be believed,
rather than (the truth) things have to be believed to be seen.

MIND THE MIND

If you correct the mind, the rest will fall into place
Lao Tzu

Become consciously aware of where your thoughts are focused. Listening to, watching, or being engaged with disempowered static frequencies of fear, issues, dramas, problems, challenges and inner critic or confusion blocks the stream of life supporting information that is trying to make its way to you. We are free when we become the neutral observer in our life without having to play out dramas and intrigues.

Quieting the mind is essential.
Entertain joyful thoughts about those experiences
you truly want to have and enjoy.

MEDITATION

Meditation is a deep state of relaxation that trains the mind and supports an inward focus. Practice anywhere to tune in to alternate states of consciousness, receive messages, visions, answers to questions, and explore the unseen and unknown. Here are simple suggestions for beginning a practice of meditation.

- Initiate SEEN.

- Choose a specific location to meditate—preferably not where you work, sleep or exercise.

- Make sure you will not be disturbed by phones, visitors, animals, etc.

- Early mornings are a great time to meditate, the world is quieter, energy is fresh and the mind uncluttered.

- Set aside a specific time to meditate each day.

- Place candles and other spiritual paraphernalia in the room to help you feel at ease.

- Find a way and position that works for you. Try sitting, lying, eyes closed, eyes opened as different ways to meditate.

- Once the mind quiets, put all your attention to the feet and then slowly move your consciousness up the body (include your internal organs).

- Enjoy the stillness.

- Once your practice is complete, spend 2-3 minutes feeling grateful for the opportunity to practice and your mind's ability to focus.

- Read books and use CD's to assist in learning more about meditation.

Insights may be intuitive or an inexplicable sudden gift of spirit. They can be triggered by a dream or a thought, come to you in meditation or while walking or sleeping at the sacred place. The sound of bird's call, the appearance of an animal or the words of someone else floating on the air can be the portal through which you discern your purpose, life's work, future, or deeper identity.

ASKING FOR ASSISTANCE

Invisible dimensions are available to help and requesting assistance is our responsibility. Walking, sitting, standing or lying—practice and use this example of how to connect with the invisible world and ask for assistance.

- Initiate SEEN.

- Call in your higher power (Christ, Goddess, God, angels, allies, ascended masters, healing masters, Eternal Divine Self, guardians, saints, etc.) and ask them to be present with you.

- State that your heart is open and invite your higher power to come rest in your heart—enter your energy field—speak to you through your mind or show you symbols or visions.

- Silently name everything you are grateful for in your life, all that you love, enjoy and cherish. Be thorough and take as long as needed.

- Silently name all you are confident about in your life, those things you know you will bring to fruition—the creations or dreams already set in motion that you know will happen.

- Make requests for what you desire to draw into your life—healing, awareness, well-being, change, enlightenment, clarity, etc.

- Feel the nutrients of the earth and the essence of what is desired flowing into the energy field and body. Direct the energy to any part of the body, mind or soul that would benefit from deep nurturing and healing.

- Images, colors or words may be given. You may suddenly get a bright idea or see an option you overlooked previously.

Information comes to us like puzzle pieces we eventually assemble. Allow the pieces to be given—the complete answer may not appear all at once.

IDENTIFYING PURPOSE AND INTENT

Any time in our lives can be used as a platform for change, personal growth, healing, clarity or renewal. When we visit sacred places, our purpose may simply be to enjoy and experience a new place—or, we may want something specific from our sacred journey. Our priorities will organize themselves according to our purpose and intent.

Here are examples of intentions expressed by spiritual explorers:

- make life changes

- gain clarity on: relationship, career and/or health

- receive next steps

- let go

- to heal—physical, emotional, spiritual

- receive life purpose

Knowing what you want to receive from your time at sacred places helps to direct the energies to that purpose. Your great powers of healing and transformation will align with the energy of the places visited to produce the desired results.

Before entering a sacred place intend to connect deeply.

DIVINING TECHNIQUES

Sacred places invite us to explore divining techniques (develop our inner knowing and psychic abilities). Divination is the ability to foresee, gain insight into a question or situation or be inspired. For thousands of years, diviners have worked with deep sensitivities and a heightened sense of awareness, used divination tools, read signs or omens and spoken with supernatural beings. Divination practices vary throughout the world by culture, religion and individual proclivities.

Your ability to discover, foresee or predict something, as if supernaturally, requires a shift in focus and the use of abilities we all have. You may have more finely tuned abilities in certain areas and it is practical and recommended to explore various ways of divining.

Trust the information you receive.
Ask to be shown and, shown more clearly.

Presented here are divining techniques for the Spiritual Archaeologist. If you feel drawn to know more about divining techniques, or feel you have a gift that needs support and development—acquire books, CD's or take an interactive class to develop your intuition. If you feel confident, just dive in—trusting you will be guided and given the information you are seeking at sacred places.

Work with several methods to find your strengths and identify your comfort zone. The material here is intended familiarize the reader with tools used by Spiritual Archaeologists. It is not within the scope of this book to transmit in-depth training. Information on Spiritual Archaeology trainings and events can be found in the back of this book.

DOWSING AT SACRED PLACES

Dowsing has been around as long as humans and is a type of divination or clairvoyant ability. A dowser can search for anything by projecting an intent or question and receiving confirmation or non-confirmation through their dowsing devices or bodily felt sense. We already know the answer and the emanations from our body and nervous system motivate the movements of the dowsing device to provide the response. Dowsing enables us to out-picture our inner knowing.

Dowsing devices such as Y-shaped or L-shaped rods, pendulums or the body itself and can be used to locate ground water, lost objects, gemstones, buried metals, ores, oil, to answer questions, measure chakras, vortices, portals and specific energies at sacred places.

Right and left-brain integration is a benefit of dowsing; it demands that we remain open intuitively as well as alert rationally. Exploration of our inner environment as well as the outer environment can be accomplished with dowsing as we tune in to the world of intuition, feeling and the sacred. Following are a few suggestions outlining how dowsing can be used at sacred places:

- communicate or receive guidance from angels, allies, ancestors, guardians and beings at sacred places
- find places where the energy field alters human consciousness— power spots and vortex sites
- locate underground water lines and springs—high energy places
- find ley lines and the directions in which their energy flows
- determine whether a ley line or water line has a positive or negative effect on what lies above or over it
- identify locations where events took place
- identify locations of healing
- find ancient ceremonial locations
- locate portals, interdimensional doorways and gateways
- have specific questions answered

BODY DOWSING

Below are techniques that use the body and do not require the use of a device. Practice by asking the body questions as you go through your day. For example: *Should I invest time in this project? Should I go for a walk right now? Is it a wise to let this person become a friend? Is the new project I am being offered beneficial for me? Is this relationship ideal?* You can ask the body anything, anytime.

Listening, being silent, feeling the sensations in the body, allowing yourself to be led to a particular spot or location is a kind of dowsing done without a device. When traveling to sacred places, having this skill in place will be most valuable. Body dowsing can be relied upon to answer questions and give direction.

The body can be used as a pendulum that will sway one way for yes and another way for no (back and forth or side to side).

- Stand and place the feet hip width apart.

- Close the eyes and ask the body to show you its *yes* and then, show you its *no*.

- Do this every time you decide to body dowse, since the direction of movement could change.

- Ask your body a question to which you know the answer is *yes* (like..."is my name ___?).

- Ask the body a question to which you know the answer is *no*.

- Continue with the question to which you desire an answer from the body.

- Trust the answer you receive.

- Thank the body.

THUMB AND INDEX FINGER DOWSING

- Create a loop with the thumb and index finger.

- Place the other thumb and index finger together in the loop and connect these two loops creating a chain with these fingers.

- Ask what is *yes* and try to pull the fingers apart.

- Ask what is *no* and repeat the process of trying to pull the fingers apart.

- In one instance, your fingers will lock tightly so you cannot get them apart. In the other instance one loop will slip through the other, separating the chain.

- To confirm this method is working, ask questions you know the answers to.

- Ask the questions you would like to have answered.

- Trust the answer.

- Thank the body. Easy!

RUBBING THE FINGERS TOGETHER DOWSING

Gently rub the thumb and index fingers together. You may experience a silky smoothness, roughness, up and down, side-to-side or other signal as you:

- Ask to be shown a *yes*.

- Ask to be shown a *no*.

- Check responses by asking questions you already know answers to.

- Ask the questions you would like answered.

- Trust the answer.

- Thank the body.

DREAMING AT SACRED PLACES

Stories of dreaming at sacred places appear in legends about sacred wells in Ireland, Scotland and England, where a goddess was the overseer. Dreamers sought answers to relationship questions: *When will I marry? Will I find true love? Should I remain in this relationship?* The goddess of the well would answer the question through a dream.

Water symbolizes the subconscious or super-conscious mind, what is hidden. Dreaming at sacred places, particularly near water, is highly recommended as a way to gain insight, determine next steps and clarify our current life situations.

Find a quiet place to sleep and dream undisturbed. Program and direct the path of your dreams:

- Initiate SEEN.

- Focus on an intention for your dreaming.

- Formulate a clear question.

- I program my dreams to bring me an answer to the question:

- I program my dreams to acquire information about my next career steps.

- I program my dreams to show me how to heal:

- I program my dreams to reveal information about my relationship with:

Be prepared by having a notebook or other recording device by your side so you can record your dreams the instant you awake. Dreams, like multidimensional experiences, are momentary, fleeting and easily lost if we are distracted for even a brief moment upon waking.

TELEPATHY: "I SPEAK AND LISTEN"

Thought transference is the easiest way to describe telepathy. Practice, and you will be surprised at how often you are already using telepathy to communicate. Animals are highly telepathic and they like to receive images rather than words. Babies, little beings that are new to our world, have their full telepathic abilities intact. Engage a baby in telepathic communication—and watch their face light up; they may even start laughing. Here are some telepathic messages we can use in our everyday encounters.

- I recognize you.

- I honor you.

- You are greatly loved.

- I love you.

- You are beautiful and brilliant!

- I am so happy you are here.

- You excel in all you undertake.

- You are a gift to the world.

Telepathy can be used to send messages at any time to anyone. Practice sending loving and uplifting messages to friends and business associates. Before going into a meeting, send messages of love and good wishes and your intentions for beneficial outcomes for everyone. Become aware of telepathic messages being sent to you.

CLAIRVOYANCE: "I SEE"

Clear seeing or vision is the nature of clairvoyance; including the ability to see the aura or energy body of a person, place or thing. This type of seeing does not emanate from the physical eyes, but from an inner sight. Practice this with a partner who can present questions. Below are two ways to access clairvoyant abilities. Practice with each and see what is comfortable for you.

Example #1

- Initiate SEEN.

- Close the eyes and focus inward. Bring your attention to the area at the back of the head or base of the skull.

- Imagine the area behind the forehead on the inside of the head as a clear white movie screen. Some people like to imagine the screen somewhere in front of the forehead outside the physical body. Either way will work.

- Ask, or have someone else pose a question.

- Allow images generated at the back of the skull to be projected on the forehead. These images might include objects, colors, names, words, numbers, scenes and may have particular meaning to you or the questioner. You may be given a series of images.

- Describe and speak them.

- You or your partner will have interpretations of these images. Have fun with this.

Example #2

- Initiate SEEN.

- Close the eyes and look upward, accessing the area at the top of the head.

- Imagine you can open this area (known as the seventh or crown chakra) and create a funnel-shaped conduit that spans out from the top of the head. In this way, we open to Source.

- Ask questions and wait for responses. Images, words or thoughts, colors, shapes, phrases or objects may appear.

The art of interpreting the images develops over time and through experience.

CLAIRAUDIENCE: "I HEAR"

Clairaudience is likely to be most appealing to those of us who think in words. This is not hearing with our physical ears. Try the following exercise:

- Initiate SEEN.

- Focus your attention inside the head.

- Direct the focus of your hearing to an area above the ears.

- Words, sounds or other type of language are experienced as an inner dialogue—like talking to the self.

- Write or speak what you hear.

CLAIRALIENCE: "I SMELL"

Our sense of smell is a magical time machine, connecting us with pasts into antiquity and the wealth of information that lies there. Smell, scent or olfaction is an ancient sense embedded deep within our primal response system. The right aroma can evoke vivid, whole body sensations that help us recognize life partners and choose friends. Smell assists us to instantaneously recall memories and can transport us back in time to experience a scene from the past.

Have you ever heard anyone say: *Every time I smell* _____, *I remember* _____? Smells trigger memory more than hearing or seeing. The smell of a ripe peach can bring us back to a summer day in an orchard long ago. The scent of a pot of soup cooking on the stove wafting its aroma throughout the house may bring a sense of peace, nurturing, happiness or wellbeing. The scent of candles and incense transports us inside a cathedral to an ancient ceremony.

A sniff of something on the air and we suddenly remember events we have forgotten for years, maybe lifetimes. These smells influence our moods, health, and work performance.

Using our sense of smell at sacred places is an excellent way to connect more deeply. A rock, tree, plant, the earth itself—all have a scent—and that scent carries upon it the memories of times past and dimensions beyond this one.

The use of essential oils at sacred places is recommended. Use essential oils from plants native to the areas visited. The plants from which they were extracted carry the earth's memory. Use the oils during meditation, spirit communication or any time a deeper connection is desired.

- Place a drop of essential oil on the forehead or heart.

- Place a drop of essential oil in the palm of the hand, rub the hands together and cup the hands over the nose and sniff the essence of the plant.

Clairalience signals us about people and events and is a means of communication from the spirit world to us. Messages of smell are sometimes spontaneous and we can also ask for this type of information.

- Initiate SEEN.

- Use essential oils as a transport system.

- Focus your attention to the heart center.

- Ask for any scents to be presented to you that are relevant to your exploration.

CLAIRCOGNIZANCE: "I KNOW"
Did you ever *just know* something? Dozens of these small enlightenments guide us through our days and support us to make decisions—like which line to stand in at the grocery store. Our knowing may facilitate a quicker checkout, put us next to someone we need to meet, or in earshot of a conversation we need to overhear for our own benefit. We simply *know* where to be. We do not question this type of knowing.

CLAIRGUSTANCE: "I TASTE"
A flavor or taste on the tip of the tongue that reminds us of a person or event. We can ask to be given the taste of a thing, some place or event and it will trigger a broader sense of the experience.

CLAIRSENTIENCE: "I FEEL"

Sensitivity and silence enhances our feeling abilities. Being in touch with how something feels in the body is an excellent indicator. A clairsentient psychic may take the hand of a client for a moment to connect and receive impressions—to *feel* what is going on.

- Initiate SEEN.

- Ask a question or have someone else ask.

- Notice how it feels—scan the body for any signals.

- What does your body tell you?

PSYCHOMETRY: "I TOUCH"

The hands are the sensory system used in psychometry—we touch an object to receive impressions. Metal objects, like jewelry, are excellent to practice with as the metal holds the vibration of wearers. Antique jewelry may have had more than one owner—see if you can tap into the person who originally acquired the piece. Try this with other objects too—an article of clothing, a pen, artifacts. It is best to practice with objects that are not your own, or objects of antiquity that have a history to reveal.

Practicing with another person can provide valuable responses and comments. Exchange impressions you receive from the objects you are examining and clarify each other's findings. An outing to an antique shop can be fun. There you may have the opportunity to interact with a number of different objects.

- Initiate SEEN.

- Hold the object in your hand(s), close your eyes and see what images, words, or other information comes to you.

- Speak it out loud if you are working with a partner, or write it down if you are working alone.

If you are in a location where touching the object is not possible, place the palm of your hand(s) a few inches or more away from the object, close your eyes, relax and breath. Connect with the object through that little heart chakra at the center of the palm of the hand. The impressions you receive will offer clues and entire stories or events for your consideration.

RETROCOGNITION: "I REMEMBER"

Retrocognition is a sudden experience or knowledge of past events that could not have been inferred or learned of by normal means. You might be left wondering: *Did it happen in a dream? Did the psyche travel backward to get the information?* We can look into and perceive the past:

- Initiate SEEN.

- Close your eyes and shift your focus to inside the head.

- Look with the inner eye in every direction and ask which direction to focus on to see the past.

- Images, colors, numbers, or entire scenes may be given. If what you are seeing is not clear, ask for greater clarity, a sharper image.

PRECOGNITION: "I KNEW IT"

Precognition is knowing or being aware of something to take place in the future. This can happen spontaneously. Practice looking into the future with this exercise:

- Initiate SEEN.

- Close the eyes and shift your focus to inside your head.

- Look with the inner eye in every direction, asking which direction to focus on to see the past.

- Allow the images to flow in, collect them, write them down or speak them.

- Answers can be quickly presented.

ASTRAL PROJECTION: "I TRAVEL"

The ability to separate the astral (spirit) body from the physical body and fly or travel to other locations is known as *astral projection*. We leave ordinary reality and enter multidimensional reality to travel. Deep meditative states and altered states enhance this ability. It is best to be guided through the process of astral travel.

IV.
PRACTICAL
SHAMANISM

PRACTICAL SHAMANISM

Shamanism is an integration of the physical and spiritual realms of existence and is based on the knowledge that all life is interconnected.

The terms *shaman* and *shamanism* are overused and improperly allocated to medicine people and other practitioners in various cultures. Specific practices by shamans and other medicine people at sacred places are endlessly varied—originating from different cultures and belief systems worldwide.

Practical shamanism requires the development of sensitivity, heightened states of awareness and a connection to all life. To be able to enter into multidimensional reality and commune with spirits at sacred places, it is necessary to embrace a shamanic awareness of the world in which we live—to respect and nurture all life.

Practical shamanism establishes a foundation for multidimensional awareness and communication.

Practical shamanism is a way of being and seeing supported by a deep sensitivity to the Self and the Earth and a willingness to connect with and consciously use the energy of the cosmos. This basic foundation enables the Spiritual Archaeologist to explore the invisible realms of existence. The basis of practical shamanism as outlined in this book relates to connecting with sacred places and the beings inhabiting them. As we nurture our sensitivity we solidify the platform for our experience of this and other realms of existence.

Shamanism is an earth based spiritual practice that cuts across all faiths and creeds and reaches into the depths of ancestral memory. Shamanism was practiced long before organized religion came into being. The belief systems, symbolism and cosmology contain gods, totems and beings who take different forms based on their cultural place of origin.

> *He (the Shaman) is a self-reliant explorer of the endless mansions of a magnificent hidden universe.*
> Michael Harner

The shaman is a human bridge between the unseen realms of guiding spirits and this world; present time—Now. Shamanic practice requires full presence in the Now, as you cannot be a bridge to a place you are not present in.

The word *shaman* originated among the Siberian Tungus (Evenks) and literally means *s/he who knows*. Shamanism predated Christianity as the dominate religious practice for humanity reaching as far back as 2.6 million years ago. Today, the word *shaman* is liberally applied to medicine people of many indigenous cultures throughout the world. Some of the defining skills shamans practice and have been credited with include:

- divination
- the interpretation of dreams and visions
- healing
- astral projection
- enlightenment

- the ability to contact the spirit world while in an altered state of consciousness

- acting as an intermediary or messenger between the human world and the spirit worlds

- knowing the entire universe to be alive and interconnected

- mending of the soul to restore the physical body

- acquiring solutions to bring positive affects to their community

- bringing guidance for others

- restoring balance to people and environments

- birthing transcendent energies

Totem animals figure strongly in the practice of shamanism and it is believed that all animals bring teachings. A shaman can imitate and/or take the form of a particular totem animal during a ritual or ceremony. Teachings of a particular totem animal may become part of the shaman's medicine—that which is shared with others. The ancient use of other totem items such as rocks or crystals is common among shamans as they are believed to have an animating spirit and special powers.

The first prophecies were the words of an oak, and that everyone who lived at that time found it rewarding enough to 'listen to an oak or a stone, so long as it was telling the truth.'
Plato— *Phaedrus*

Some societies believe shamanic abilities are inherited and can be passed from generation to generation. Others believe shamans must be "called" to serve—apprenticing themselves to accomplished shamans. Others believe the shaman is naturally initiated.

Being struck by lightning, a personal psychological crisis, a near death experience or a serious illness can initiate the shaman. A shaman may be transported to the spirit world, experience a dismantling or dismemberment and then a reconstruction. Initiatory experiences may bring specific visions, imagery, or revelations of magical powers.

Many cultures had their shamanic practices wiped out with the spread of Christianity, as temples were destroyed and ceremonies were outlawed. Campaigns against "witches," often orchestrated by the Catholic Inquisition wiped out European shamanism during the Middle Ages and Renaissance. Spanish colonization brought Christianity in its wake, instrumental in the destruction of local traditions. Medicine people were executed as "devil worshipers" in the Caribbean and Central and South America. The English Puritans in North America conducted periodic campaigns against individuals perceived to be *witches*.

Christian missionaries still, today, carry out attacks on shamanic practitioners in third world countries. Missionaries in the Amazon defaced historic petroglyphs just a few decades ago. The list goes on and the idea that *my god is better than your god* remains a prevalent theme causing death and destruction worldwide. Shamanism continues to survive in indigenous communities and other locations throughout the world.

Spiritual Preparation

Spiritual preparation for visits to sacred places are matters of personal beliefs and preferences—there is no right way to do this. Devoting time and energy to an upcoming sacred place journey or ceremony does have a payoff—we position ourselves to receive the benefits we are seeking.

A shaman or medicine person takes time to prepare the body, mind and spirit for ceremonies and journeys to sacred places. The purpose of spiritual preparation is to amplify and sustain the vibration of our entire being. The vibration and frequency we hold is the magnet attracting what we desire, others and those in the unseen dimensions. Great care is taken to purify and enrich the being on all levels. When we take the time to prepare our whole being, communication with the spirit world and sacred places happens easily and effortlessly.

Preparation might include spending time with an elder who can initiate a you into the ways of communicating with the spirit world. Teachings about offerings and ceremonies, customs, ancestors, rituals, and other dimensions are shared. Often, a journey to a sacred place is a rite of passage intended to reveal a spiritual or life direction. In our modern society, these traditions may be limited or non-existent.

There are none greater or less than you in all the worlds.
Sam Tchakalian

Spiritual Archaeologists may frame their journey and visit as a rite of passage or place it in any context they wish. You are encouraged and supported to contact the spirit world. Following are some examples of traditional ways of preparing for a spiritual journey:

- meditating

- fasting

- elimination of alcohol and drug use

- sensory deprivation

- praying

- journaling (including dream journaling)

- reading inspirational books

- becoming familiar and comfortable with solitude

- reviewing the past and reasons for making the journey

- contemplating the meaning of surrender

- preparing the self for a symbolic death and rebirth—the old self dies and we anticipate renewal through the birth of a new self

- singing and dancing

- ritual practices

- chanting and voice harmonics

- ceremonial bathing (to cleanse physically and spiritually)

- using altars or medicine bags before or during a journey

- ceremonial fires

SENSITIZE

I want you to learn a new way of using your mind that
liberates you from 'facts' and 'beliefs' by focusing on your own
direct, moment-to-moment experience.
This is where your real power resides; this is the way to wisdom.
Christian de Quincey

An inward focus is crucial to personal fulfillment and to commun-
ing with invisible worlds. Relaxing and stabilizing the physical body,
quieting the mind, and centering in the heart (SEEN) prepares and
supports the Spiritual Archaeologist at sacred places.

TUNE IN

Insight into and communion with the unseen, other dimensional realities and the beings inhabiting them is the core of Spiritual
Archaeology. Tuning in to higher frequencies requires an inward focus
and the elimination of distractions.

Our world is saturated with abundant, unfiltered incoming information and background noise from electronic devices. We have been
conditioned to hook up to predominant cultural information sources
that do us no good, do not add to our wellbeing and are often disturb-
ing, fear-based and detrimental to our health.

Streaming images and chatter flow through televisions, radios and
other electronic media and spout off in almost every environment we
enter. Channels provided by consensus reality dull the senses, instill
unwanted programs, influence our thinking and feeling bodies and
condition us to a fear-based existence. Captive in a kind of trance, disconnected; the sounds of the earth, animals and plants and the messages of spirit are diminished or lost.

The need to be constantly entertained
diminishes our ability to connect with, be enlivened by,
and in flow with the natural world.

There are other channels—channels emanating from an infinite domain of expanded consciousness. Silence opens us to higher
thought and unlimited realms of information. Our inner knowing is

strengthened. We can create and choose stories we want to tell ourselves—stories reflecting a reality experience we strongly desire to live out, free of fear, disease and destruction.

Silence and listening tunes us in to what stillness has to reveal. Our connection with ourselves, the natural world, our planet and other people becomes the primary information source.

PRESENCE

Leave the mind vivid, without any constructions, just as it is.
In the space between old and new ideas, discover the natural, unfabricated,
luminous and knowing nature of the mind unaffected by thought.
H.H. Dalai Lama

We receive more from life and relationships when we locate ourselves in the Now. The subtle energies and beings at sacred places require our full presence. In any situation where full presence is required, alcohol and drug use is not recommended.

Release any psychological assessment, processing, thinking of the past
or future or other distracting mental activities.

Land, waters, rocks, temples—whatever exists before, beneath or around us is alive and vibrating with life force. Use the Heart-Opening Breath to clear the mind if it becomes cluttered with thoughts, assessments and ideas.

CLOSE THE EYES

Simply close the eyes to eliminate visual data and distractions. Our inner focus is made active. Look up to the crown area of the head or focus on the area between the eyebrows and slightly above.

BREATHE

Exhale fully. The breath is automatically pulled into the body, filling the abdomen and chest. Deep breathing relaxes, centers and connects us to the earth. Send out a vibration of love to everything and everyone around you.

SILENCE

Let us be silent, that we may hear the whispers of the gods.
Ralph Waldo Emerson

Silence allows us to drop deeply into ourselves. When we eliminate speech and other sounds, we experience heightened awareness in all our other senses. Move your focus out of the head and into the heart. Silence opens the receptivity mode.

Silence is a multidimensional prayer, supporting our
inner knowing and divining abilities.

LISTEN

Listen with the entire body. Listening to the sounds of birds, wind, trees, animals, people and our footsteps on the earth allows us to consciously merge with the rhythms of the universe, become part of nature. Listening can be cultivated through silence and meditation.

BODILY FELT SENSE

Check in with the body periodically and see what messages
it is putting forth. Honor the wisdom of the body.

Our bodies are accurate sensing devices. Take time to scan the body and notice any areas of tingling, stiffness, pain or other signals. Focus your attention inward:

- Bring your attention to the toes, then the feet.
- See into and feel the entire body—move your consciousness upward from the feet through the entire body, including the organs.
- Notice any areas of tightness, pain, etc.
- Does the body want to lie down, sit or stand?
- Is there a feeling of exhilaration, tiredness, strength?
- Any aches, stiffness, or holding?
- Become aware of and tuned to the body's signals.

Interpretations about what these signals mean are left to the individual. Each of us carries unique pieces to a much larger puzzle; each of us will see, hear and feel very different things. Every piece is important.

LET GO

When we believe things are a certain way and will remain so, we block the flow of new information and possibilities.

Release the overlays of history, legend and interpretations, assumptions and conditioning. These are someone else's findings. Let go of any preconceived ideas based on what has been read or heard. Allow sacred places to reveal themselves. What you see, intuit and experience will be unique and will tie into your life, dreams and purpose.

TRUST

Trust may be the single most important element of any exploration into the invisible realms of life and sacred places. Spiritual Archaeologists acquire information based on a heartfelt sense, visions, feelings, intuition, dreams and personal connections made with ancient and prehistoric sacred places and cultures. Completely trust your insights and recognitions.

What is yours will come to you.
My Father

OPEN THE HEART

Use the Heart-Opening Breath. Focus your consciousness in the heart and move slowly and softly to support the vulnerability of the open heart

BECOME CHILDLIKE

Approach sacred places as a child might—openhearted, in wonder, and enthusiastic to make discoveries. Ask to be shown and made aware of anything the site or guardians want to share.

BE RECEPTIVE

Receptivity is critical in welcoming new information. Staying open to what is presented and what you intuit supports the continued flow of information. Should you experience discomfort or an uncomfortable moment, stay with it and be willing to discover and receive what the experience has to show you.

OPEN THE HANDS

Opening the hands is a gesture of receptivity and willingness. There are little heart chakras in the palms of the hands. Maybe you have seen paintings or pictures of saints or holy people beaming light from the hands? Opening the hands with the palms facing forward enables us to beam our healing light out through the center of the hand and fingertips. Cast a path of light ahead of you, announcing your approach. This posture enables sensory information to gather and penetrate; it enhances our ability to connect and receive.

WALK SOFTLY

Consider each footstep a prayer.

Our feet are part of our multi-sensory system, and it is our feet that connect with the earth as we approach and explore sacred places. This is a practice to integrate anytime you are walking on the earth. It is particularly useful walking up hills or mountains:

- Slow your pace.

- Become aware of the heel touching the earth first, then the toe.

- As the left foot touches the earth, inhale and draw in the energy of the earth, the light.

- Flow this light through the body, revitalizing, renewing and restoring all parts of the being.

- As the right foot touches the earth, heel to toe, exhale and release any old, tired energy from the body. The earth receives this old energy and can use it (as it is not judged as good or bad) to revitalize itself. A healing exchange is created by this action

CONNECT WITH THE EARTH

*The shamanic practice of merging mind, body and spirit
with the Earth's vibration opens a pathway for the direct flow of energy,
feelings and healing, opening the Self to deep awareness.*

Primary to our explorations of sacred places is making a connection with the earth. The earth is the keeper of great wisdom, renewal and healing and we can practice this connection anytime, anyplace in the world.

- Initiate SEEN.

- Lie face down, on your back or sit on the earth.

- Focus on the Heart-Opening Breath.

- Feel the earth beneath you, breathing with you.

- Experience your body as weighing a million pounds, sinking into the earth.

- Merge your energy field and body with that of the earth and relax into the wellbeing that is available.

ALTERED STATES

Mystics and shamans, among others, consider altered states a necessary discipline in their quest for the *divine, truth,* or *reality.* Our ordinary waking awareness is only one aspect of consciousness and viewing our lives from this single-point perspective can limit our field of vision and operation.

It is not necessary for the Spiritual Archaeologist to seek altered states of awareness through plant medicine. Sensitivity to the self and environment will produce an altered state automatically.

As visitors to sacred places we may experience a kind of altered state, a shift in awareness or consciousness. Naturally induced altered states take many forms, but most commonly, we may find ourselves in a partial dreaming and waking state. We may be unable or unwilling to speak, feel dizzy, hot or cold, enter a trancelike state, experience a shift in focus or attention, become disoriented, or relaxed into a previously unknown peaceful state.

Our life experience is enriched by entering altered states—
other planes of existence become known
as we travel backwards and forwards in time.

Altered states open us to visions, voices or sounds, stimulation of the chakras, out-of-body experiences, speaking in tongues, psychic phenomena, trances, ecstasy, communication with other beings, and feelings of union with spiritual reality and earth. Our particular state of personal growth is often reflected in these experiences.

Alteration of our senses comes naturally as we develop
our sensitivity. Silence initiates the process.

Following are some of the traditional means used to produce temporary changes in consciousness and/or its content. These techniques produce transitory manifestations that are part of our longer-term development:

- specialized breathing

- sensory deprivation

- meditation

- yoga

- drumming

- dancing

- chanting

- ecstatic dance

- hypnosis

- sonics

- voice harmonics

- plants and chemicals

Both positive and negative forces are present in nature and in every realm of existence—physical, psychic, mental, emotional, and spiritual. We enter the astral or psychic world when we transcend the physical plane, entering a slightly more ethereal form of matter containing influences and entities ranging from lowest to highest.

Impressions of all thoughts, feelings, and actions of humankind since the dawn of time are located on the psychic or astral plane.

We draw impressions from the psychic and astral plane by affinity and similarity of vibration. All our thoughts and feelings come to us through the medium of vibrational resonance. What criteria can one use in evaluating and choosing among available techniques to alter our consciousness?

Select ways to access altered states that feel natural and safe for you. Don't explore out of your depth or without proper guidance and support.

Discernment, wisdom and selectivity about our interactions are crucial when we expand our awareness to include the invisible. We can take control of what we call forward and engage with by requesting that only the beings of the highest vibration and light make themselves known. We can also shield ourselves from any unwanted energies.

Guidance and support is highly recommended when plants or chemicals are used to access astral realms. Someone who is experienced and capable of stabilizing and directing diverse spiritual energies and traveling to and from astral realms would make a perfect guide.

When we return to ordinary reality, it can be challenging to remember all that has happened in an altered state. Keeping records of these experiences as they occur is important, as much is lost in trying to recall them later.

TALKING WITH SPIRITS

All living things have wisdom, a spirit and something worthwhile to communicate. A transfer of energy takes place when we communicate with the spirit world. Shamanic practitioners make a link from the spirit world into this world by becoming a conduit for guiding spirits.

The energy or transmission of a spirit can affect the individual practitioner, another person, a group or the whole world.

Spiritual Archaeology involves establishing relationships with invisible worlds and the spirits who inhabit sacred places. Establishing a relationship with the spirit world will proceed as any other new relationship might. Who are you speaking with and what do they have to offer? Trust must be in place to be able to work with spirits—use your instinct. This is an interview process and you may have to speak to more than one spirit to find your ideal ally or allies for your explorations.

- Initiate SEEN.

- Use your notebook to record the interaction.

- Begin writing each question and answer that follows.

- Ask if there is someone available who can answer your questions. Wait for a confirmation—Yes or No.

- Ask if this is an evolved spirit (doesn't have an ego and isn't involved with opinions, personal agendas and agendas of the world). Have the spirit tell you a little about who they are. An evolved spirit will not seek to control you or interfere with your free will.

- Ask the spirit whether they are a guide or ancestor or other (angel, ascended master, past life friend, faerie, saint, etc.)

- If an ancestor or relative appears it is important that that have gone to the light—reconnected with higher knowing. Ask if this is so. If not, decline the engagement, thank them, and ask for someone else to step forward.

- Ask if the spirit has a personal agenda.

- Ask whether the spirit has your best interest at heart.

- Does the spirit know what they are talking about and are they capable of responding to the particular questions you might have?

- Ask if they will identify themselves by name.

- Notice how you feel—is this spirit a loving presence with your best interest at heart? Just as you would in any relationship, use your discernment.

HOW DOES SPIRIT COMMUNICATION FEEL?

Spirits vibrate at a different frequency than humans and energetic changes occur within us when we work with them. Being sensitive to how the communication feels in your body will let you know if there is a potential for overwhelm. Often, the most powerful experiences with spirit are very subtle, releasing healing, clarity and information over time rather than right in the moment.

It is important to feel grounded in any communication with the spirit realm—use SEEN to stabilize and flow any excess energy through your grounding cord into the earth. Our physical being may alter to communicate with spirits. An example might be looking upward with the eyes closed, off to the right with the eyes open. You may also feel slightly dizzy, light headed, very present and grounded, or highly charged. Notice any physical changes and relax into them—we all have different ways of opening and sustaining communication with the spirit world.

WHAT CAN A SPIRIT TELL ME?

Spirits can act as healers, advisors and teachers, sharing energy and information that has value In many areas of our lives. A spirit teacher often has valuable insights into our unconscious motives, the core of issues and relationships, what steps might be next, or the source of a physical or emotional condition. Always ask for clarification and more detail. Be receptive to what is given, even if it is not what you want to hear. It may be necessary to take a risk and flow with new information.

Speaking with spirits is a relationship that we develop over time. The trust factor will also develop as we see the results of information given. Be clear when asking questions of a spirit teacher. In the spirit world all life experiences are considered beneficial as they all have great teachings to impart. You may not be after another learning experience. The question: *Should I be in relationship with this person* might more clearly be asked as: *Will being in relationship with this person fulfill my deepest desires for happiness and joy?*

HOW DO SPIRITS COMMUNICATE?

Spirits are all unique and may set up a means of communication we did not expect. Smells, words popping into you head, visions, feelings in your body and sounds are some of the ways of spirit communication. The following practice, *Writing with Spirit*, is an excellent way to initiate contact and carry on a dialogue.

WRITING WITH SPIRIT

The spirit world is available to speak with us and we can initiate communication. *Writing with Spirit* can be used to access information about a sacred place we visit, our relationship to it, or any other questions we may have.

This writing will feel natural and have a flow to it that does not involve the thinking process. Words come quickly into the mind and you need only transcribe them. Once a response to a question is complete, formulate another question. Begin this easy and powerful practice at home and use it anywhere and anytime:

- Reference the *Talking to Spirits* section of this book and use the process outlined there for establishing the relationship before continuing.

- Choose a quiet place where you are comfortable and will not be disturbed.

- Have a notebook, journal or recording device available.

- Initiate SEEN.

- Close your eyes and formulate a question.

- Write the question in your notebook.

- Write a response to your question—word by word as it is given.

- Allow the words to flow without editing or judging.

- Eliminate any ideas that you are making it up.

- Continue to ask questions and receive answers and to write.

This is not a time to review what you have written; it is simply a time to ask questions, receive and record the responses. You may feel exhilarated at the speed and clarity of the responses you receive. Following are sample questions to begin a dialogue at a sacred place:

- Is someone here with me and willing to respond to my questions?

- Have I been at this site in the past?

- What is the true nature and purpose of my journey to this place?
- What have I come here to learn, see, understand or know?
- What are the lessons I can take with me from the distant past that will cast a positive reflection in my life at this time?
- Where is the strongest energy available to me at this site at this time?
- Is there anything I should consider leaving behind or ending as I move forward with my life? Is the energy to let go of mental, emotional, physical or psychic?
- What are some of the components of my new life and reality?
- What am I not seeing?
- Is there healing energy available to me at this site?
- Where is it located?
- How should I access that energy?
- Are there any messages specifically for me from this site?

Be as creative and specific as possible with your questions. The questions you formulate may include some of these and others more specific to your personal quest.

INTERSPECIES COMMUNICATION

Plants, animals, rocks, waters, mountains—all natural forms on our planet are alive. We can connect with these beings and exchange information. If you have a pet, using telepathy to send mental pictures to them is a good way to practice. An artifact from a site can be asked about its origin, maker, purpose or age. An example of how to address other species follows:

- Refer to the *Entering Sacred Places* section of this book to begin.
- Initiate SEEN.
- Create a dialogue as follows using these or similar words:

   Sacred (mountain, stone, tree, water, being, etc.) who, like myself, holds the memory of all times—I honor you as a magnificent and life-giving being with vast intelligence and

*wisdom. Although we are in different forms at this time, I
know we are one, sharing the experience of being on earth.
I ask you to share your wisdom with me, and I invite you
to take from me any information that is of value to you. I
am grateful to have this opportunity to connect with you
and exchange information. I extend my love, gratitude and
blessings to you.*

- State your intention—what you have come to learn, give, realize, transmit.

- Ask questions and receive answers. Write them down if possible.

- Enjoy the dialogue.

- Remember to offer a gift of gratitude and blessing upon completion.

VOICE HARMONICS

*Modern science is now in agreement with what the ancient mystics
have told us that everything is in a state of vibration, from the electrons
moving around the nucleus of an atom, to planets and distant
galaxies moving around stars. As they're creating movement, they are
creating vibration, and this vibration can be perceived of as sound.
So everything is creating a sound, including the sofa that we're sitting on,
or this table, or our bodies. Every organ, every bone, every tissue,
every system of the body is creating a sound.*
Jonathan Goldman

Our natural voice is a powerful tool for altering our consciousness, clearing the mind, healing the body, connecting with invisible worlds and amplifying awareness. Practice anytime, at home, in the car, lying down before or after sleeping. The following exercise initiates sonic frequency in the body. Sound is the ancient and future language beyond language emanating from infinite domain. Create and enjoy different vibrational frequencies.

- Find a comfortable place where you can sit or lie down undisturbed.

- Initiate SEEN.

- Take a deep breath in and exhale the sound *A*

- Play with vibrating and moving *A* from the abdomen to the heart, throat, inside the head. You can direct the vibration of *A* to any part of the body.

- Change the position of the mouth, open wide and close a little at a time to produce different sounds.

- Move the tongue to the roof of the mouth, bottom of the mouth curve the tongue. All these positions of the tongue produce different frequencies.

- Have fun exploring how to modulate the sound of *A* and move it throughout the body.

- Place you hand over the belly, chest, arm, forehead, top of the head....while concentrating the sound in that area. Feel the vibration.

- *A* and all subsequent sounds in this exercise can be directed to any area of the body in need of healing or revitalization.

- Work with the other vowels: *E, I, O,* and *U* (pronounced *uu* rather than *u*—like the vowel sound in "who").

SONIC MEDITATION
Set aside a minimum of fifteen minutes a day to meditate sonically. Use the format above and become familiar with feeling of being in a sonic resonant field of your own creation. Voice harmonics produce a relaxed, altered state perfect for the exploration of sacred places.

Arriving at Sacred Places

To enter the spirit-mode takes courage. You have to dedicate your life to yourself. This is not an egocentric view, more an act of prayer unto yourself. It does not make you more important than the world you live in, you just become the world you live in.
Stuart Wilde

Indigenous people acknowledge and interact with invisible worlds and the beings that inhabit them and base their knowledge of the past on their ways of knowing (oral traditions), legends and myths. They believe the places their ancestors occupied are alive, not dead—and the ancestors still inhabit them. Sacred places await our visit and the sensitivity and respect we embody, honors all.

ENTERING SACRED PLACES

The energy fields of sacred places are finely tuned to recognize and receive visitors who have been appearing for hundreds or thousands of years. While the crowds may storm through the gateway the minute it opens as they would on a sale day at a department store, an attitude of reverence is one of the gifts you can bring to sacred places. Basic guidelines follow:

- Be it temple, pyramid, mountain or stream, we meet our ancestors, guides, allies, god, goddess, higher power, and the Eternal Divine Self when we visit.

- Pause in the general area of the site or at the entryway. When visiting a old friend, we would not barge through the door without announcing ourselves. The same is true at sacred places.

- Hesitate a few moments and initiate SEEN.

- Focus on the heart center and clear the mind.

- Observe any customary ways for entering or approaching the area. For example, a Buddhist Shrine should be circled clockwise three times before taking a place of prayer or meditation.

- Intend to establish the deepest connection possible with the site.

HONOR THE GUARDIANS

All sacred places have guardians who oversee and monitor comings and goings. Even if you don't believe such things, it is customary and wise to honor the guardians before entering a sacred place.

A few years ago, I met a man in South America who told me a story. Juan had no spiritual leanings and beliefs about the invisible world. Having lived his entire life with the view of a sacred mountain, he knew he would visit the mountain one day. Years later, he bought a new truck and felt confident about making a journey to the mountain. He set off and, try as he might, he lost his way several times and found himself driving away from the mountain rather than toward it. Juan was determined to reach the mountain and minutes after he turned on to a different road, the axle on the truck broke. He had to call for help and abandon the journey.

Some months later, still enthusiastic about visiting the mountain, Juan enlisted the services of a local shaman. The shaman had an old car and together they struck out on roads that appeared to be impassable. From time to time, the shaman would stop the car and get out. He said prayers and made coca leaf offerings to rocks or trees, or in unmarked places alongside the road. These, Juan was told, were the guardians of the sacred mountain.

The shaman was able to maneuver the old car over the rough terrain and eventually position it and the passengers within 600 feet of the base of the mountain—much closer than Juan had ever imagined possible.

Juan looked at me while telling the story and said, "I did not believe in these things, invisible guardians and spirits of a place. After making this journey with the shaman to the sacred mountain, I know they do exist and if they are not honored, access may not be possible."

In our excitement to enter the site, we don't want to overlook this primary step. Take a few moments to acknowledge the guardians, ask for passage and protection and express gratitude. Here is an example of a simple greeting to extend before entering:

- Guardians of the ancient cities and sacred lands....especially, (name the site).

- My name is:

- I ask your permission, protection and blessing to enter here today.

- My purpose for this visit is:

- State your intention: (for example: prayer and thanksgiving, renewal, inspiration, healing, exploring, clarity, remembrance).

- I ask that you guide me to the location(s) at the site that will help me to achieve my purpose and assist me to fully receive the benefits of this visit.

- I thank you for preserving the energetics of the site and allowing me to enter. I am grateful for your presence here.

- I offer you my blessing and gratitude.

It is not important to use these exact words, but do acknowledge the guardians, speak your name, your purpose, and thank the guardians for access.

OFFERINGS

Offerings can be presented to the guardians before entering and again at any particular location within the grounds.

Determine, in advance, what offering might be traditional or customary and comply with the custom or tradition. Buddhist temples in Asia sell incense to visitors to burn in a large receptacle before entering. Candles are sold outside churches and cathedrals. Visitors place them in a holder that is provided inside the building and pray. Coca leaves are used in Peru in specific ways by Curanderos. Tobacco and cornmeal are used by Native Americans. These biodegradable and earth-based offerings are used in a tiny amount (for example—a pinch of cornmeal) and placed in an inconspicuous place.

Unless instructed as to the proper use and placement of offerings, do not leave visible offerings at the sites. If you have a biodegradable offering, prepare it as follows.

- Place the offering in the hands and place the hands over the heart.

- Use the Heart-Opening Breath to transfer your love and essence into the offering.

- Extend the offering to the earth or guardians.

Do not leave anything visible at the site or bury objects. Foreign objects, including crystals and stones left at the sites interfere with the frequency and intention of the sacred place.

LEAVE IT WHERE YOU FIND IT

Dirt, rock, stones or artifacts—whatever exists at a location is to remain at that location. Upon the return of several crystals to the Kogi in Columbia, they were able to facilitate four rivers to spring from the earth. The stones, and artifacts, according to the Kogi, are part of the place they came from. Taking anything away from an area, including many objects that now rest in museums, compromises the well being of an area.

FINDING YOUR PLACE(S)

Hold an intention to make a clear and strong connection with the site and to be led to the perfect location for your purpose.

Walk slowly, feeling each footstep connect with the earth. Stop, sit or stand periodically as guided to do so. Wander through the site, feeling the way rather than following along or rushing. Stop to meditate or to gaze over the site. Sense and feel the perfect place to be: a cave to sit in, a place to lie down on the earth, sitting or standing beside a wall. There is no right way to do this—trust your inner knowing.

An individual place of power at a sacred place may not be anywhere near the main site, temples, shrines or ceremonial areas.

Dowse to locate your perfect place and take the time needed to explore and sense.

CEREMONIES

Sacred places have been the repositories of ceremonies for millennia. A ceremony can be anything from a simple, silent prayer to a complex and elaborate production. When we visit sacred places, we step into the aura or field of many ceremonies of the past. What do we want to add to this, if anything?

Words or prayers of acknowledgment, truth, and gratitude spoken from the heart are always an appropriate ceremony.

Respect for indigenous people, their land, rituals and ceremonies is essential. Overlaying ceremonies of our own is not recommended or welcomed at many sacred places. An experienced local ceremonialist, shaman or medicine person will know how to address the site, call forth the guardians and energies, make the appropriate offerings, and assist you to receive value from the experience.

V. SEDONA,
ARIZONA, USA

SEDONA

Sedona is a natural site—
its power emanates directly from the earth.

The car mechanic is a brilliant numerologist, the contractor is an alchemist, the landscaper is a master astrologer, your doctor is a talented psychic, the restaurant owner is a crystal skull expert and your neighbor is definitely an alien. The town shuts down by 9:00 PM and most people don't know exactly how they landed here. After spinning in the vortexes for a while, they can't remember exactly where they thought they must be going. The air is clean, artists are ever inspired, people are friendly and the Humane Society has one of the nicest buildings in town.

Most people have heard of Sedona, Arizona—its a destination. Some stay a couple hours passing through Uptown as tourists, coming from or going to the Grand Canyon. Others succumb to *red rock fever*—they feel Sedona is their true home and decide to rent or buy a house and stay on.

Sedona is a natural site—its primary elements are red rock spires, canyons, pinnacles, buttes, mesas, high desert, mountains and flowing water. Surrounded by the Coconino National Forest with Oak Creek flowing down the canyon through it, Sedona is a visual and natural wonder.

Many of the buttes of the Red Rock Country evoke qualities of guardianships, of wise and eternal presences watching over the land.
Nicholas Mann, Sedona, *Sacred Earth*

Ancient astronauts would have seen swirling spires and mammoth whimsical red rock sculptures rising from the desert floor, and figured—this would be a good place to land. They would have known—the earth is happy here, she has made something special—an eye dazzler and feast for the senses. We are heartened and uplifted, seeing the beauty and majesty of Sedona's red rock landscape.

The earth vibrates at an astonishing frequency and the magnetic pull of invisible forces and energy fields is conducive to wellbeing and enhanced psychic abilities. The heart feels at home, inspiration flows, and visitors and residents alike are recharged by Sedona's unique energy.

Invisible impressions of prehistoric visitors sweep through the dimensions. Healers, shamans, medicine people, seers and wisdom-keepers leave their imprints as ceremonies, prayers and intentions. These interactions represent a significant contribution to Sedona's continuing magnetism and power.

Temples, beings, writings, giants, goddesses or gods, legendary heroes, mythical places, animals and ancient civilizations appear and disappear on the red rocks with the changing light of day. Visions and dreams, stories of the past, present and future, symbolic meanings and windows into other worlds twinkle in the setting sun, at magic time, in Sedona's red rocks.

As in the past, people visit Sedona to receive their next steps, to gain clarity, make life changes and to refresh, renew, restore and revitalize. Sedona and the entire Verde Valley is alive with history, rich in culture, refined earth energy, legend and spiritual significance.

Sedona's Sacred History

Traditional Archaeology tells us Sedona and the Verde Valley shows evidence of habitation going back at least 11,000 years, naming prehistoric and nomadic hunters and gatherers as the first inhabitants. Sinagua, Hohokam, Mogollon and Anasazi people all passed through the area.

Pottery shards, corn cobs, remains of dwellings and charred cliffs are some of the evidence of people living in the Sedona/Verde Valley in the past. Native Americans consider Sedona a sacred place, a ceremonial site, and I have heard it said that people should not be living in Sedona. Years ago, a Native American man walked into a shop and informed the owner that his business was doomed to fail (it did), as it was built over a ceremonial site. There are specific locations up and down 89A where it seems businesses cannot make a go of it. Local lore attributes these rapid incarnations to events that have taken place on the land in the past. Sedona is a place of emergence and beginnings.

THE SINAGUA

Between 500 AD and 1425 AD the pre-Columbian cultural group known as Sinagua occupied an area between the Little Colorado River and the Salt River. The name *Sinagua* (seen-aug-wah) means *without water*—referring to the prevailing condition in their area of habitation. Those who lived around the Flagstaff area, above the Mogollon Rim, are considered Northern Sinagua. The Southern Sinagua lived in the Verde Valley and Central Arizona.

Pit houses were the earliest Sinagua structures found. Pueblo type habitations appeared later, consistent with those found in other ancient cultures throughout the Southwestern United States. They also built their homes under the natural rock overhangs in the area. The Sinagua survived as hunter-gatherers and grew squash, corn, and beans. They were skillful weavers of cotton and makers of red clay pottery, which they traded with other groups in the area and as far away as Mexico and the Pacific Coast.

Approximately 5,000 Sinagua inhabited the Verde Valley and at the peak of their civilization they vanished. Many believe they migrated north to the Hopi Mesas; some may have intermarried with the newly arrived Yavapai. Some believe the reasons for their disappearance were religious—they were told by Spirit to leave the area. Others theorize they are still here, living in another dimension.

THE YAVAPAI-APACHE

The Yavapai-Apache Nation is a living treasure of Sedona and the Verde Valley. Theirs is a long and diverse history tied to Sedona's red rock country. The area they originally inhabited spans beautiful Oak Creek Canyon, the mountains to the south and west, the White Chalk Hills of Camp Verde, and eastward to Clear and Fossil Creeks. They may have been living in this area at the time of the Sinagua (approximately 1100-1300 AD).

In February of 1875, approximately 1500 Yavapai (Wipukyipai) and the Apache (Dilzhee) were taken from their homelands (Rio Verde Indian Reservation) to the Indian Agency at San Carlos, Arizona. The United States Army, acting on a presidential decree, led a brutal march in harsh weather through flooded rivers and mountainous terrain. Hundreds of lives were lost.

The United States government became the beneficiary of several thousand acres of treaty lands promised to the Yavapai and Apache by removing them from their ancestral lands. When the Yavapai and Apache returned to the Verde Valley, after being released from 25 years of internment, they found that Anglo settlers had taken up residence in the fertile Verde Valley. There was no longer a place for the Yavapai and Apache, yet they remained within their homeland area until a reservation was reestablished in 1909.

Two distinct tribes (the Yavapai and Apache) became known at eh Yavapai-Apache Tribe in 1934 and, in 1992 they voted to become the Yavapai-Apache Nation. The tribe has been able to buy back some of their land in the Verde Valley.

The footsteps and songs of the Yavapai and Apache can be felt and heard through the canyons, along the rivers, out in the desert landscape and beneath the glistening stars at night. Their ceremonial sites and sacred lands have been greatly compromised by development in the area.

NEW ARRIVALS IN THE AREA

The Spanish arrived in the late 1500s. Gold was discovered in 1863 and, the first white settlers arrived in the remote Verde Valley in 1876.

By 1902, only 20 white settler families lived in the area. A postal station was opened by T. C. Schnebly whose spouse's name was Sedona. That's how the city got its name. Artists, writers and other creative types have always been drawn to Sedona and those who made a home here include Walt Disney, Max Ernst and Dorothea Lang.

NATIVE AMERICAN STORIES

Legends and myths are told repeatedly, and in each telling the story may shift slightly from the original. The following examples are stories from the Hopi and Yavapai tribes close to Sedona.

THE HOPI

Prophecies are passed by Hopi Elders from generation to generation through oral traditions, dances, artifacts and references to ancient stone pictographs and tablets. Different clans have different stories to tell. One well known prophecy of the Hopi states, "When the Blue Star Kachina makes its appearance in the heavens, the Fifth World will emerge." The Hopi name for Sirius is Blue Star Kachina. It is said the Day of Purification will come when the Blue Star Kachina dances in the plaza and removes its mask.

The Red Earth is sacred and important to many Native people. The Book of Hopi, written by Frank Waters talks of the migration of the Hopi from the First to the Fourth World, which we are in right now. Sedona may be the fabled "Red City of the South," the legendary Palatkwapi, considered to be a paradise by the Hopi. The warm climate, fertile soil, river and creeks present a welcoming and life sustaining environment and the stunning red rock landscape holds a special fascination for all.

Jesse Walter Fewkes, a pioneer of archaeology in the Southwest, believed the Sedona/Verde Valley area was the Red City of the South. Hopi legends say the Red City is somewhere in the far Southwest, and some think it may be as far distant a Palenque in Chiapas, Mexico. To this day, its true location has not been affirmed.

The Red City was a great cultural and religious center for the Hopi who traveled from the Red City towards the Hopi Mesas. Walking the "Good Red Road" in the other direction, toward the Red City, signified a return to the world of spirit, a pilgrimage or vision quest to a site where they could commune with ancestral spirits.

The Hopi migration legend goes on to say that Palatkwapi was destroyed by a great flood that wiped out the Third World. The inhabitants of the Red City fled to the North along the Palatkwapi Trail to Homolovi and farther to the Hopi Mesas. The Hopi claim that Palulukang (Kukulcan in Mexico) the horned or plumed serpent (known as Quetzalcoatl throughout Mesoamerica) who was said to inhabit the sacred cenote known today as Montezuma's Well, was responsible for the tremendous rainstorms that brought on the deluge, destroying the Third World.

Tuzigoot National Monument located in Clarkdale, Arizona is a possible location for the actual village of Palatkwapi.

THE YAVAPAI

A Native American creation story tells of Sedona as a place of emergence of the goddess Komwidapokuwia (or Kamalpukwia), which means "first people with medicine" or "old lady rock." Another creation story told by Mike Harrison and John Williams (Yavapai/Apache) states:

> We came out at Sedona, the middle of the world. This is
> our home. We call Sedona "Wipuk." We call it after the rocks
> and the mountains here. All Yavapai come from Sedona. But,
> in time they spread out.

The Yavapai are native to Sedona and the group of the Yavapai living in Sedona call themselves the Wipuka, highlighting this connection.

According to Yavapai legend, the *Lady of the Pearl* was sealed in a log with a woodpecker and sent from Montezuma's Well to prepare for a Great Flood. For days and nights to follow, it rained incessantly and the waters of the flood rose covering every landform on Earth. The rain finally stopped after 40 days, and when the water receded the log came to rest in Sedona. A beautiful young maiden was freed from the log by the woodpecker. The Lady of the Pearl was guided by the woodpecker to the summit of Mingus Mountain. Her people had given her a white stone or *Pearl* for protection and this she carried with her. On Mingus Mountain she met the Sun and they fell in love. She bathed in an enchanted and magical pool in Boynton Canyon when she returned to Sedona. After this, the *Lady of the Pearl* became pregnant and birthed a daughter who became known as the *First Lady* and mother to all the Yavapai people.

Three sites are mentioned in this creation story: Montezuma Well, Sedona (Boynton Canyon) and Mingus Mountain. Water is also a principle element of the legend siting both the sacred cenote at Montezuma's Well and the sacred spring in Boynton Canyon. The cliff dwellings at Montezuma's Well, in Boynton Canyon, and the hilltop settlement at Tuzigoot may have existed as sacred structures. Pilgrims seeking inspiration, healing, guidance or wisdom may have lodged at these dwellings for a time, just as today's visitors to Sedona and the Verde Valley find lodging to undertake their spiritual journey in the area.

Sedona Stories

Connection and communion with the planetary energetic
vibration in Sedona enhances insight and
a higher frequency inhabits the body and mind.

All nature of folklore, ancient and modern, circulates around Red Rock Country. These *Sedona Stories* include the presence of multidimensional beings, extraterrestrials, folktales, myths, legends, superstitions, traditions and mysteries. Magic seems possible, if not ordinary. The roots of Sedona as a spiritual Mecca run deeper than present times with the stir about vortices.

WHERE'S THE VORTEX?

"Where's the vortex?" might be the most frequently asked question by visitors to Sedona. Several years ago, a clairvoyant named Paige Bryant studied the energy system in Sedona. She is responsible for citing the locations that people flock to when in Sedona—Bell Rock, Cathedral Rock, Airport Mesa and Boynton Canyon. Clairvoyants, healers, medicine people (native and nonnative), spiritual guides and locals have identified other locations of powerful energy.

The entire area is a vortex, or energy center. The red rocks have an uplifting and clarifying affect on visitors and locals. People feel good just being in Sedona and return repeatedly to recharge. The refined earth energy has a positive influence on the brain and creates a feeling of wellbeing.

Meditating or connecting deeply at a vortex or energy site opens a portal to tap into higher dimensions. Both humans and the Earth have at least 12 layers of subtle bodies along with a current physical body. Being close to an active chakra of the earth (vortex), we are able to grasp the multidimensional and ever changing nature of life.

On the planetary grid system map (Becker Hagens 1983) it is noted that Sedona is one of the five areas in the Northern Hemisphere indicated as a positive healing energy vortex. What does that mean; how does it operate and what will happen when we visit a vortex site?

Benjamin Lonetree, scientist and engineer (www.sedonaanomalies.com) states:

> *Vortex centers have unique physical properties. Iron-bearing basalt (lava deposits) runs through sandstone, creating magnetic vortices. The red rock spires in the Sedona area are natural formations of this kind. They can be imagined as negatively or positively charged electrodes, carrying current. Water, iron, silicon (granite) and traces of copper, silver and gold in the earth create a natural device that attracts and amplifies this electrical energy. The earth discharges this energy, creating a physical or metaphysical occurrence. In other words, the measurable energies rising from the earth in Sedona touch back down into the earth at a location nearby.*
>
> *Humans embody oxygen, silicon and iron in their blood, cell salts and glands that rest in the positions of the chakras. The correlations between these materials of the earth and the human body build a harmonic resonance. The vortex energies of Sedona amplify the human psychic centers allowing for a connection between the different dimensions. Access to these unseen dimensions can come as dreams, visions, heightened awareness, mental clarity, a sense of well being, communications with spirits and beings in other dimensions, instantaneous healing, expanded possibilities, emotional release, stepping out of linear time or other upgrades to the human experience.*

Dowsing is an excellent way to locate vortex energy and find a location that is right for you.

ENERGY SYSTEMS

Ancient people knew that wherever the earth's energy gathered was a sacred place. As we relearn and remember the ancient shamanic and medicine ways based on a relationship with the earth, our attraction to these places is intensified. Sacred places we see today are often built over sacred places of the past—the energy has sustained many incarnations. The reciprocal relationship we establish with the earth enhances us in direct and subtle ways. Temples, pyramids, churches and other centers of spirit are examples of places built on energy systems. An example of an energy system would be the confluence of two underground streams of water.

Powerful vortexes or energy systems are the earth's chakra system. People and the earth both have a major and a minor chakra system. Ancient and modern mystics use song, sounds, and ceremonies to keep a chakra or chakra system open, cleansed, and properly working. Understanding how energy is generated, measured and maintained is central to our decisions concerning the use and conservation of energy—personally and on the planet.

Another energy system is outlined by Gary David in his book, *The Orion Zone*. He tells us the Orion star system sits above the sacred places in the Southwest, USA and there is also a chakra system for the area. He states that the sixth chakra is named as the San Francisco Peaks in Flagstaff, Arizona. The energy in transformed through this sixth chakra and cascades down into the Verde Valley.

The Verde Valley corresponds to the seventh chakra—the place where the cosmic self and individual self merge. The seventh, or crown chakra, is our place of connection with infinite domain, enlightenment, bliss and transcendent states of being. Ultimate divinity is realized through the crown chakra. It is also the location where the spirit leaves the body at the time of death—making its way back to the stars.

According to this system, Tuzigoot in Clarkdale, Arizona, may be the location of the crown chakra. This viewpoint is appealing and reaches far beyond the magnetism of the vortices as one way to understand the magnetic pull of Sedona and the Verde Valley for spiritual seekers. Many people attracted to the area are seeking advanced spiritual truths and a connection with their higher self.

HEALING IN THE RED ROCKS

People who visit Sedona may be seeking healing and often find it. Whether physical, emotional or spiritual healing, the red rocks are a perfect place to let go of the past and receive a new vision. There are talented healers in Sedona who know how to use and direct the energies. Healing takes place at the moment we are ready to let go. A healer opens the conduit for this to occur, the choice is made, and a healing takes place.

EXTRATERRESTRIALS AND SPACESHIPS

Legends from many cultures tell us about star people who came to earth in a distant past. Inter-dimensional portals are like tunnels leading from Sedona to other dimensions and, it is said, these portals are frequented by extraterrestrials passing from one dimension to another.

A camera documented a bright green object flying from the South at high speeds on in January on 2012. The green object maintained a steady horizontal pattern and continued north. In the mid-90's, during a two week time, extraterrestrial craft were seen (no telescope necessary) zigzagging and then dropping rapidly into different locations around Sedona. UFO sightings in Sedona are as common as weather reports.

Internationally known paranormal and UFO researchers spend extended periods of time in the Sedona area, or locate permanently to expand their knowledge and work. All kinds of things show up on photographs or videos—images and objects that cannot be seen when the photographer take the photo. I once saw a video taken by a tourist on Airport Mesa of a spaceship. It was clear as could be. I don't believe he was particularly hunting for a ship, but he certainly did find one.

CRYSTAL CITY

Another aspect of Sedona and any sacred place has to do with what lies beneath the earth. Sedona is considered a crystal city due to both the crystalline rock underlying the land and the visions people have had of crystal temples in the etheric realms.

Looking out over the expansive valley, you can see glowing red rock temples. Do you have to use your imagination to see these things? Yes, and No. Some people, for instance, believe that there is a crystal temple underlying Bell Rock. Certainly, anyone who is open to Sedona's wonders will see powerful visions.

CEREMONIAL SITE

Sedona is an earth temple—a repository for the ceremonies, prayers, songs, dances, intentions, healing, music, visions and dreams of local and visiting shamans and medicine people. There is an energy emanating from the earth itself, kept alive by those who continue to revere Sedona. We know today, just as the ancients did—that whatever we energize in a sacred place will have more power and reach.

Stories tell of tribes from as far away as Mexico to the South and Canada to the North traveling to Sedona for ceremony and ritual. They sought visions, messages and clarity for the coming times in their lives. Present day visitors also want to know "what's next?" The veils between the worlds are thinner in Sedona, visions come easily and people feel closer to Source.

ROCK ART

Stories of the distant past are incised and written on stone around the world. A wealth of rock art exists in Sedona and the Verde Valley, telling stories of the lives and beliefs of those that came before. These sites are extremely important and fragile and should be enjoyed without touching the rocks.

PORTALS

Sedona, Arizona is one of the most famous cosmic portals in the world with more reports of inter-dimensional, multidimensional and unexplained phenomena than anywhere else on earth. Cosmic portals, gateways or doorways between dimensions, inter-dimensional doorways, stargates, 2-way tunnels, curtains of light, cosmic bridges or cosmic wormholes are some of the names given to portals. Portals often occur with energy vortexes—where energy seems to surge up from the earth or into it.

The boundaries of a portal are not clearly defined—they can be a few inches across or span hundreds of feet. Realities merge at a portal; the edges blur where one reality meets another, there can be unusual temperature changes, colors are more vivid than surrounding areas and a sense of enhanced or refreshing energy may occur.

Digital thermometers, EMF meters, dowsing rods and pendulums are devices used to locate and measure portals.

Spiritual Archaeology in Sedona

Sedona is a natural earth-based sacred place. Here, the Spiritual Archaeologist will explore the natural terrain. Earth, mountains, archaeological sites, waters and stones are the components of the area and each will be addressed separately. Choose what appeals to you and plan your exploration.

Read and refer to Section VI of this book on *Outdoor and Site Etiquette* before venturing out on the land. Sedona offers excellent opportunities for the Spiritual Archaeologst.

EARTH

New ways of perceiving the world and reality are revealed in Sedona.
Beliefs and expectations play a part in forecasting our experience
and the earth connection we make facilitates it.

The earth carries the vibration of ceremonies, dancing, drumming, prayers, hopes and dreams of all who have visited before. The rich and enduring impressions of shamans, medicine people, healers and ceremonialists linger in the canyons, out on the trails and permeate the red rocks. Connecting with this vibrant energy is easy—find your quiet place and check into Sedona.

Using your divining abilities, you may find a location to explore right near your home, hotel or the center of town. One does not have to go far to tap into the energies of Sedona. The power spot or location that is uniquely yours is not likely to be anyone else's.

SPIRITUAL ARCHAEOLOGY—EARTH

If you do nothing else while you visit Sedona, make time for this exercise. You will be greatly rewarded.

- See the book section: *Entering Sacred Places.*

- Lying down or sitting on the earth insures an excellent connection. Lying face down is ideal, if possible.

- Initiate SEEN.

- Concentrate on the Heart-Opening Breath. Sync your breath and heartbeat with that of the earth.

- Imagine that your body weighs a million pounds and feel it sink more deeply into the earth with each breath.

- Allow yourself to drift into the vibrant healing energy of the red earth.

- Refer to the section of this book on *Interspecies Communication* to dialogue with the Earth.

SACRED MOUNTAINS

Our Sacred Spirit put us on these Six Sacred Mountains (the sacred mountains of the Four Corners Area of the American Southwest). And the Six Sacred Mountains are not outside us—they are inside.
Katherine Smith Yinishye, *Big Mountain Navajo*

Mountains and mountaintops stretch from the earth and reach toward the stars—a desirable location for the ancients and a destination for life after death. Taller than the surrounding landmass, a mountaintop has always been considered a place closer to Source. To reach this pinnacle is, at once, a challenge, a relief and, finally, a victory. The air is purer, cleaner and thinner—vision is enhanced. Surely, being at such heights is being in the place of the gods.

Mountaintops are closer to the sun, our definitive and ever-present source of power and light. Civilizations around the world have worshipped the sun as god, and great temples were built to honor this life-giving golden light representing the creator.

Mountains are places of deep connection with the Self and Source. We climb a mountain to gain a more finely tuned perspective, achieve greater clarity and initiate healing or change. On a mountaintop our ability to meditate is enhanced, and we experience elevated thoughts.

According to Taoist belief, the mountain is a medium of communication between people, the immortals and the primeval powers of the earth.

Practitioners of Feng Shui (also known as Geomancy) consider mountains to be powerful sites of telluric power, a sacred force of energy running through the earth itself. This energy is also known as dragon energy. According to these practitioners, the dragon current is of two kinds, yin (feminine) and yang (masculine), and mountains are regarded as embodying the yang.

Spending time at the heights lifts the spirit and broadens perspective. If you have a mountain visit on your agenda, plan to spend time once you reach the summit. Lie down on the earth and connect with the strength and wisdom of the mountain. Meditate, pray or do whatever you feel will connect you more deeply. Know that you can leave the past behind and walk into a new beginning as you make your way down the mountain.

Spiritual explorers are naturally drawn to reaching the heights, and climbing mountains helps to transcend this earthly existence; if just for a little while. Those attracted to mountains in the Sedona area have choices:

- Bear Mountain—6,541 feet

- Lost Wilson Mountain—6,762 feet

- Wilson Mountain—7,122 feet

- Lee Mountain—6,592 feet

- Munds Mountain—6,834 feet

Contact the U.S. Forest Service for up-to-date information on trail conditions and other important things to know before you go: http://www.fs.usda.gov/coconino/

MOUNTAIN CLIMBING IN SEDONA

In Sedona, mountain paths can be rugged with many loose stones and tiny rocks. Be well prepared for your climb. The climate is warm or hot during the day with temperatures dropping dramatically once the sun goes down.

Here are some suggestions for the mountain climbing enthusiast in Sedona:

- Bring layers of clothing—a lightweight fleece and rain jacket that rolls up for easy transport can be lifesavers.

- The climate is dry and drinking water is essential, lots of water.

Dehydration happens quickly and is very dangerous.

- Wear shoes with deep cut treads. Flat-bottomed shoes offer no protection or support on the rocky trails and no traction to prevent rolling and slipping.

- A pair of hiking sticks are excellent to bring along.

- Bring your cell phone in case you need to call for help.

- Let someone know where you are going and when you expect to be back. This can be a friend or someone at the hotel where you are staying. People get lost out there, and cell phone service is not always available.

- Pack along snacks like protein bars, fruit and nuts.

- Bring sunscreen and/or hat. The sun is strong in Sedona and stronger as you climb higher.

- Bring a small pocket mirror—in the event you are lost or hurt with no cell phone service, signaling aircraft with a mirror can bring help.

- Pack a small flashlight in your bag.

- Avoid climbing on delicate sandstone and limestone structures, spires and buttes—they break apart and crumble easily causing erosion and extreme danger for the climber or hiker.

- Contact the United States Forest Service to learn of trail conditions, closures or other current information that will be valuable to your climb. You can acquire a map from the USFS Red Rock Ranger District office (8375 Ariz. 179, just south of the Village of Oak Creek or write P.O. Box 20429, Sedona, AZ 86341-0429; phone 928-203-7500.

- Read the section of this book on *Outdoor and Site Etiquette*. This will clearly outline what you need to know about being in the outdoors.

- Bring your notebook (paper or electronic) or recording device.

SPIRITUAL ARCHAEOLOGY—SACRED MOUNTAINS

- The journey up a mountain provides an ideal opportunity for the practice of Spiritual Archaeology.

- Ascending the mountain is a time for *letting go* of anything and everything you no longer need to hold or carry—beliefs, ideas, conditioning, relationships or whatever you are now ready to release.

- Each conscious footstep is a prayer. Walk slowly—with the left foot (heel to toe placement) draw the nutrients and healing from the earth. With the right foot release the essence of old, tired energy into the earth. The earth gratefully accepts this gift of energy and converts it to nutrients.

- Feel the cleansing in your body, mind and spirit as you release the old and make way for the new.

- With each inhale, imagine bringing a sparkling golden light into all aspects of the self, revitalizing, restoring and healing from the inside out.

- Once at your destination on the mountaintop or somewhere along the way where you feel drawn to stop, prepare a comfortable place for yourself where you will be undisturbed.

- Initiate SEEN.

- Read the section of this book on *Writing with Spirit* if your choice is to communicate with the mountain. Meditate, pray, or use your divining skills to access information and receive the messages of the mountain.

- Refer to the section of this book on *Interspecies Communication* to dialogue with mountains.

- Keep a record of your experience, questions and answers.

- Descend from the mountain slowly and carefully. This is a time of integration, bringing in the new and receiving expanded vision or reality.

- As you walk down the mountain, visualize and feel yourself with the desired changes and upgrades in place.

The journey up and down the mountain allows for an expansion and healing of the self. Use it wisely; it is good medicine.

ARCHAEOLOGICAL SITES

We have a few precious archaeological sites in Sedona and the Verde Valley. Although archaeological sites are often referred to as *ruins*, Native Americans and other indigenous people around the world consider these places to be alive and inhabited by their ancestors. Approach and visit these sites with the respect you would accord to an elder or wisdom keeper. Step lightly, listen carefully and express gratitude.

GUIDELINES FOR VISITING ARCHAEOLOGICAL SITES

Due to vandalism, graffiti, and other destructive acts, we have increasingly more limits placed on our fragile archaeological sites in the Verde Valley. Visitors are asked to maintain a consciousness of stewardship when visiting these sites. Here is a list of guidelines for visiting an archaeological site:

- Every part of the site is extremely fragile—walls, structures and the areas around them. Climbing, sitting, standing or leaning on the structures can cause irreparable damage.

- Information is altered forever when we remove artifacts or rocks from the sites. It is not only the archaeological reference that is compromised, but the site and land lose part of their vibration and spiritual integrity.

- We are fortunate to have petroglyphs and pictographs remaining in the area—some are thousands of years old. These outdoor museums reflect stories of the past and should be viewed and felt rather than tampered with. Any type of marks, writing, painting, touching, altering or engaging with these ancient writings creates irreparable damage. Generations to come are denied their experience with these places due to unconscious acts by visitors. Archaeologists lose valuable information. There is no upside to this behavior.

- Take a photo of your self-standing in front of a site if you need to have a reminder that you were there. Writing one's initials on a rock wall, wood-post, historical building or any monument is egotistical, inconsiderate and downright stupid.

- During your travels, you may spot artifacts and be inclined to move them or stack them together in another area. There is a story being told in the location of the artifacts and once they are moved, a piece of the past is destroyed forever. Digging, dislodging, removing and piling up of artifacts changes what we might learn about a location. Leave it where it lies.

- The reconstruction of past environments is dependent upon cultural deposits, including the soil on or at an archaeological site. Past environments can be reconstructed by scientifically testing the soil to reveal information (i.e. the types of plants that were used by past inhabitants).

- Carry out any trash (especially organic remains) you may have while visiting a site. Always bring an extra plastic bag to carry out trash others may have left. This is a great help in discouraging the practice of littering.

- Stay on designated trails. There are fragile desert plants and soils that are part of archaeological sites and they are destroyed when you stray from the trail. Trails are there for your protection.

- Small desert animals and snakes make their homes under rocks, in burrows and bushes. These environments are precious to the animals and we want to take care not to disrupt or destroy their homes and lives.

- Fire destroys prehistoric organic materials, ruins the dating potential of artifacts, and damages or even destroys rock art and the history left for all to enjoy and discover. Absolutely no fires, candles, or smoking should occur at archaeological sites.

- Meanings of images and symbols painted and pecked on stones are still being studied. Refrain from touching any rock art as the oils from even the cleanest of hands can cause the images to deteriorate.

- Drawing, painting, scratching, carving, and graffiti destroys rock art and obliterates the messages left to be deciphered.

- Wooden and stone buildings have their stories to tell as well. Refrain from any type of marking or carving on these structures.

- Please leave your pets at home. In their normal routine of digging, urinating and defecating they can destroy fragile cultural deposits and frighten other visitors and native animals.

- Do not ride or drive your bicycle through archaeological sites.

- Do not camp in a site or dismantle historic buildings for firewood or any other use.

SPIRITUAL ARCHAEOLOGY AT ARCHAEOLOGICAL SITES

Archaeological sites require us to be super sensitive. They are delicate environments and receive much human traffic due to tourism. Silence is a great practice when visiting archaeological site—let the stones speak to you.

- Interacting with archaeological sites is a rare opportunity to sense the past. The earth and the stones await—steeped in multidimensional memories and information. It is not necessary to touch the stones directly to commune with them.

- See book section: *Entering Sacred Places*.

- Initiate SEEN.

- Open the hands, palms facing toward the rock or structure. Vibrations, messages and images can be received while holding the palms of the hands six inches or more away from the rock or structure.

- Close the eyes and concentrate on the center of the palms of the hands as being an active receptor of information coming from the rocks or structures. You may feel warmth or a slight vibration in the palms of the hands. Allow the connection between your hands and the structure to develop.

- With your eyes closed, look up toward the center of the forehead.

- Notice if there are any colors, words, visions or messages appearing. This could take a few minutes, so take your time and be patient.

- Simultaneously, notice any signals from the body, areas of discomfort or tightness. Tune into body signals and see if there is a message there, a signal, a memory, a vision.

- Remain sensitive.

- Telepathy and other Divining Skills can be employed to connect with archaeological sites and the beautiful images on rock walls.

- If a location exists where you will be undisturbed, practice meditating and dreaming.

- Afterwards, if feasible, sit or lie on the earth. Connecting the body with the earth is always desirable. Position yourself out of the flow of traffic and away from the structures. Nearby is close enough.

- Refer to the section of this book on *Interspecies Communication* to dialogue with the archaeological site.

- Use the *Writing with Spirit* exercise to dialog with the site, makers of the images, guardians, ancestors or previous residents.

- Record your experience.

- Leave a prayer of gratitude and blessing.

SACRED WATERS
Water immediately connects us to all life; to Source.

All water is sacred. Sacred bodies of water present themselves in all sizes and shapes, covering an estimated 75% of the planet. Springs, rivers, lakes and streams crisscross our world, weaving intricate patterns above and below the earth's surface. In all cultures, the miraculous emergence of living water is seen as the matrix of life itself, and the qualities of purification, healing and regeneration naturally follow.

Water is alive, intelligent, evolving and nourishes all life.
We can plant a seed, but without the addition of water, it is unlikely to grow. We are seeds of the earth also, and with water we are nurtured, sustained, supported and thriving.

Water holds a mystery in the nature of its depths. It can be soft and embracing if entered gently and hard as a rock when we smash into it. Raging waters can destroy buildings, property and lives in an instant. Healing waters have curative powers that transcend what modern medicine has to offer. What a delicious mystery this water is!

SACRED WATER IN SEDONA

Oak Creek runs through Oak Creek Canyon, through Sedona, and down to Cornville, where it connects with the Verde River. Fruit orchards, particularly apple, were nurtured by the creek in the early days when white settlers first came to the area. The Verde Valley and Verde River Watershed attracts close to a third of the 900 species of birds in the United States and Canada—from many varieties of the miniature hummingbird to huge broad winged raptors.

The flowing waters in Oak Creek Canyon attract an abundance of animal and plant life—over a dozen species of fish, forty species of amphibians and reptiles, bird species numbering over a hundred, mammals present over fifty kinds, plants and flowers present over five hundred types. This wealth of nature is one of the many offerings of Sedona.

Water, within its liquid crystalline essence,
holds the thriving vibrations and patterns of every plant, animal,
mineral and human that has ever lived upon the earth.

Apart from the life-giving qualities of water, healing and divination are traditional virtues of water. Explorers of all descriptions visit the waters, drink of it, bathe in it or take to it in times of stress or when healing or clarity is needed or desired.

Ancient and contemporary indigenous cultures consider
water sacred and curative and treat it with great reverence.

Ceremonies and gatherings have been taking place for tens of thousands of years at water sites. Sacred places are often located above an underground stream or the confluence of two underground bodies of water. Our connection to water may involve immersing ourselves in its pure liquid crystalline essence, having a drink, sprinkling a few drops into our energy field or walking along the shoreline.

SPIRITUAL ARCHAEOLOGY—SACRED WATERS
Connecting with the water in Sedona can most easily be accomplished by a visit to Crescent Moon Park or West Fork in Oak Creek Canyon. There you can walk alongside the water through pathways and over rocks and take a dip on hot summer days.

- Refer to the *Entering Sacred Places* section of this book.

- Find a quiet spot, sit or lie down.

- Initiate SEEN.

- See and feel the flowing water washing away all that is no longer necessary to hold in your body, psyche, or life.

- Feel the fresh flowing water bringing in new energy and wellbeing—restoring and revitalizing every part of the body, mind and spirit.

- Open to what your meditation provides.

- Refer to *Interspecies Communication* section of this book to dialogue with the water.

- Refer to *Writing with Spirit* to initiate a dialogue with water.

Dreaming near water is an excellent way to receive our next steps or gain insight into areas of our lives or relationships.

- Find a place where you can lie down and be comfortable and undisturbed for some time.

- Bring warm clothing or a blanket.

- Refer to the section of this book on *Dreaming* for complete instructions.

Bathing in the waters can be a time of meditation, whether you are simply soaking your feet or immersing your full body. Healing energy is strong at water sites. Speak to the spirits of water; ask for their assistance in healing on physical, emotional or other matters.

SACRED STONES

*Stones are enduring libraries holding the ancient wisdom of
extreme human antiquity. Walk among the stones,
connect with them, listen to their stories.*

Stones of all sizes and shapes make up the mystical landscape that is Sedona. Whether you are looking at these natural structures from a vantage point or simply driving by them in your car, they have stories to tell. There are stones that reach up and become mountains, swirl into spires and peaks—while others cluster together. Many names have been given to these stone structures, and visitors may still choose other names for them. From the mightiest to the tiniest of stones, each carries a vibration and has a story to tell.

Stones have been venerated since the earliest times. Worship of stones is found in most ancient cultures, and mentions of stones are found in most of the world's religions. Stones and crystals are liquefied minerals that have hardened in the earth's atmosphere. As self-contained energy systems, they make excellent conductors for electromagnetic waves and currents.

*Stones, gems and minerals have sonic signatures
that can be read and interpreted.*

The ancients often marked with stones those places on the earth emanating powerful frequencies. Monuments of stone and circles of stone are found throughout the world marking sacred places for successive worshipers and religions for thousands of years.

Romancing the stones is an apt description of our relationship with them. The entire world of precious and semiprecious stones is another category of delight. The elaborate crowns worn by monarchs were not purely decorative. The gemstones embedded in the gold, silver or other precious metals were devices to give the monarch a clearer line of communication with Source. The spectacular jewel-studded crowns worn by monarchs, often viewed as part of the regalia, pomp and circumstance, are actually high-powered antenna reaching far into other dimensions.

There are also many beliefs and ideas about the power of crystals.

Indigenous and aboriginal people have knowledge and remembrance of their existence and use in distant pasts.

SPIRITUAL ARCHAEOLOGY—SACRED STONES

Apart from the very large stones in the landscape, there are stones of all sizes offering an opportunity for connection. Pick up a stone and hold it in your hand, or place it over the heart or forehead. Breathe and tune into the stone—see what it might have to share. Below is an outline of a process that can be used for stones of any size.

The large stone structures highly visible in Sedona are wisdom-keepers and are seen by many as actual beings. From Airport Vortex it is possible to commune with many of the most prominent rock formations in Sedona.

- Choose a red rock structure you find appealing. It is not necessary to be right next to the stone; you can speak to different stones from one vantage point. The open spaces in Sedona allow for visual contact with many of these structures.

- See *Entering Sacred Places* in the book for information as to how to begin.

- Initiate SEEN.

- See *Interspecies Communication* to begin a dialogue with the stones.

- Bring your attention to the inside of your head.

- Look upward between the eyebrows and slightly above.

- Open the crown area at the top of the head and the clairaudient center just above the ears.

- You are now open to receive messages and communication in a number of ways.

- Refer to the *Writing with Spirit* section of this book, if that method is of value during this communication.

- Refer to your research questions or use some of these:

    - Will you allow me to connect with you?

    - Is there anything you would like to tell me about yourself?

- Do you hold wisdom, healing or other energy or information that would be of value to me?

Ask specific questions relating to your circumstances. Certain rocks, like certain people, are more responsive. You may have an opportunity to be closer to a rock or sit near its base. When you feel complete, thank the guardians, the rock itself and leave a prayer of gratitude.

Sedona and other sacred places are the repositories for planetary wisdom, just as we are. When you visit or interact with the special energies of such places and their guardians, always leave a prayer of gratitude and blessing behind. Acknowledgment of the exchange that has taken place honors everyone.

VI.
OUTDOOR AND
SITE ETIQUETTE

OUTDOOR AND SITE ETIQUETTE

Natural environments are receiving more visitors all the time and many are unfamiliar with how to be on the land and preserve it. Whether you plan a day hike or a longer journey, preparation has many phases. Understanding the outdoors and our relationship to it will support us and the magnificent natural environment in which we live.

Those of us who travel to sacred places and visit the pristine forests and lands around the world are the natural stewards of these places. No rule, regulation or law has any ability or power to protect and care for these sacred places; that is entirely up to those who visit and enjoy them. Our personal role in preserving these sites is crucial to their continued existence. Worldwide, sacred places and monuments are increasingly confined due to the heavy traffic of visitors and destructive and disrespectful actions by a few.

Be Respectful

Sacred Places are the destinations of millions of travelers every year and many sites suffer damage and are negatively affected from the steady stream of visitors.

Climbing on monuments, pyramids, temples and natural sites accelerates erosion and often causes permanent, irreparable destruction. In many cases, the spirits, ancestors and guardians will be disturbed. Although climbing is often the practice at a site, and you may see others doing it, avoid climbing, whether they are hills, pyramids or other structures. Reaching the top of an ancient pyramid is not an accomplishment we need to have, especially if our only purpose is to take a picture and say we have been there.

Allow the site to change you; do not attempt to change the site. Do not move things around or take things from the area. Do not leave anything at the site, particularly anything that is not biodegradable. Unless it is clearly the custom, do not leave objects at the site, including visible offerings.

Below are basic guidelines for the outdoors that can be applied to Leave No Trace Center for Outdoor Ethics (www.lnt.org) is an excellent resource. Below is material from their site, other wilderness sites and personal experience. Read and become familiar with these guidelines.

PREPARATION – BEFORE YOU GO

- Research and know any regulations and special concerns for the area you'll visit.

- Learn about local weather and trail conditions before travel.

- Prepare for extreme weather, hazards, and emergencies.

- Bring appropriate clothing and gear for climate and areas you will visit.

- Schedule your trip to avoid times of high use.

- Visit in small groups when possible. Consider splitting larger groups into smaller ones. This reduces the impact on the earth.

- Before making a journey, visit your physician to address any concerns about your physical condition.

- Choose destinations you are physically capable of navigating.

- Learn any skills necessary to support your travel experience before you leave home.

- Learn to use any gear or equipment before making the journey.

NAVIGATING TRAILS

- Stay on the trail—protect the native vegetation and reduce erosion by staying on the trail, even if it's muddy.

- Avoid making parallel trails, cutting switchbacks or widening trails. Low-growing and tiny plants and mosses are delicate and necessary to the environment. Restoration is costly and often fails—it is better to protect the land up front.

- Let others discover wilderness on their own—never mark a new route with blazes or cairns, or litter the backcountry with flagging tape.

- Walk single file in the middle of the trail, even when wet or muddy.

- Be courteous. Yield to other users on the trail. Step to the downhill side of the trail when meeting pack animals or hikers coming down a hill.

- Use a GPS, map or compass to eliminate the use of marking paint, rock cairns or flagging.

CAMPING

- Designated camping ares are usually marked by sign posts. Camp only in designated camps, along trails, or in the location specified on your permit or otherwise indicated.

- Durable surfaces include established trails and campsites, rock, gravel, dry grasses or snow. Camp only on durable surfaces.

- Pitch your tent on established bare sites, not on the vegetation.

- Camp at least 200 feet away from lakes and streams to protect riparian areas.

- Altering a site is not necessary. Good campsites are found, not made. Concentrate use on existing campsites.

- Focus activity in areas where vegetation is absent. Keep campsites small. Disperse use to prevent the creation of new campsites and new trails.

- Avoid camping at any places where use is just beginning.

- A collapsible water carrier reduces the number of trips and trampling to a water source and allows you to wash well away from lakes and streams.

- Use small amounts of biodegradable soap for washing yourself or dishes. Carry water at least 200 feet away from streams or lakes and scatter strained dishwater.

CAMPFIRE AWARENESS

- Campfires can have a lasting effect the backcountry. Use a lightweight stove for cooking. Take along a candle lantern for lighting.

- Fires are not always permitted, check with your local forest service to determine the current situation. When making a fire use established fire rings, a fire plan, or mound fires.

- Control the size of your fire. Keep fires small. Bring your own firewood when possible or use sticks from the ground that can be broken by hand.

- Burn your fire down to ash. Put out campfires completely, then scatter cool ashes.

- Douse campfires with water until saturated and no smoke or coals are detectable.

- Cover the fire with dirt or rocks if water to douse it is not available.

DISPOSING OF WASTE

- Whatever you bring in, be sure to pack it back out. Inspect your campsite or other   areas of habitation before leaving the area. Remove any spilled foods, trash, litter or leftover foods—take them with you when you leave.

- Carry a plastic bag on hikes and nature visits and pick up any trash left by others. The psychological message of trash left on the ground is that it is OK to leave more rash. By removing trash we have an opportunity to help discourage this behavior.

- Dig cat-holes dug 6 to 8 inches deep and located at least 200 feet from any water source, camp, or trails. This is for the deposit of human waste. Cover and disguise the cat-hole when finished.

- Any toilet paper and personal hygiene products should leave the area with you.

LEAVE WHAT YOU FIND

- Examine, look, but do not touch, cultural or historic structures and artifacts. Leaving things the way you find them will preserve the experience for generations to come.

- Rocks, plants and other natural objects can be appreciated and explored, but leave them as you find them.

- Leave flowers for others to enjoy.

- Take nothing away and leave nothing behind.

- Non-native plants, no matter how beautiful should be left where they are. Do not transport these species to other locations.

- Do not build structures or furniture in the outdoors.

- Do not dig trenches or alter the landscape in any way.

RESPECT FOR WILDLIFE

- Take in the beauty and grace of wildlife by observing from a distance. Allow them the freedom to be as they are. Do not follow, approach or capture them.

- Never feed wild animals. Feeding wildlife puts them at risk in many ways. Their health is compromised, natural behaviors are altered, and exposure to predators and other dangers ensues.

- Store all food and trash securely to protect wildlife.

- Always control pets, or leave them at home. It is not safe to allow pets to run unleashed or uncontrolled—there are wild animals out there and small animals are vulnerable to attack.

- Mating, nesting, raising young and certain seasons are very sensitive times for wildlife. Stay away from their habitations and nests.

CONSIDER OTHER VISITORS

- Show respect for other visitors in the outdoors and protect the quality of their experience.

- Camp away from other visitors, respecting their private space and creating private space for your self.

- Enjoy the symphony of nature's sounds—let them prevail. Lower your voice and avoid loud voices and loud noises.

- Electronic equipment can be limited to what is necessary, like the ability to call for help if there is an emergency. Wilderness is a respite from modern technological society—enjoy the solitude the outdoors offers.

BE SAFE

- If you plan to hike or visit a remote area, be sure to let someone know where you are going and how long you plan to be gone.

- Take adequate water and whatever other supplies you might need in case of being lost or an emergency.

- Be sure to have layers of clothing for warmth, if needed.

- Determine whether the area you will be hiking or visiting has cell phone service.

- When traveling with a guide or tour company to remote areas, determine whether communication devices are in place to call for help if there is an emergency.

- Pack a small medical kit.

- What you see is what you get.

- There is no fixed reality here.

What you see is what you get.
There is no fixed reality here.

mangoes crash to the ground
splatting and splashing their juicy sweetness onto the earth
a rich jungle canopy shields the bodies
of screaming howler monkeys
while silent jaguars circle from habit

clothed in long white tunics
dark silky haired—rainforest dwelling
guardians of jungle ruins
Yaxchilan and Bonampak
where it is said the gods resided
when they lived on earth

ancient Lancandon Maya
who conquistadors never found
appear at the entry portal to Palenque, Chiapas, Mexico
place of serpents—realm of the jaguar

Palenque's Temple of Inscriptions
carved into the lush steaming jungle
climb a path and jump to an upper ledge
walk to the front—up steps to the top
slip through a black net hanging at the entry
protecting the temple from birds and bats

inside—an opening in the floor
to a steep limestone staircase
slick with moisture
frozen in time
steps more suited for giants than humans
heavy wet air slippery with Atlantean pearls
studded emeralds of knowledge
invisibly incised into the walls

at the bottom—behind a metal grate
the tomb of one who
from the stars came
ancient Mayan ruler
alien airline pilot—tunnel car traveler
Pacal Votan—Pacal the Great

in 1939 almost 1300 years later
Dr. Jose Arguelles is born
world renowned visionary, educator, author of
The Mayan Factor

Earth Ascending
The Call of Pacal Votan
an originator of Earth Day
initiator of the 1987 harmonic convergence
sparks massive renewed interest in sacred places around the
world

Arguelles invokes
star people, ancestors, extra terrestrials, extra higher
dimensionals
above—crystalline earth
below—another earth within this earth
that knows us—but we know it not
reminding us
it is between these intelligences we live

he says
we cannot survive the mistake of living in artificial time
out of harmony with the universe
indigenous people are the caretakers of the biosphere
and a whole a new society
will evolve indigenous values
into new
galactic
cultural forms
to be shared by all people as one—on Earth.

supernovas sending out cosmic messages
Pacal Votan says—Jose Arguelles says
return to natural time
avoid
dodge and redirect
override
reverse
stop in its tracks
biospheric destruction

lead a simpler life
communicate telepathically
breathe with the heartbeat of the earth

lead a simpler life
communicate telepathically
breathe with the heartbeat of the earth

ABOUT THE AUTHOR

LUMINOUS is a Spiritual Archaeologist, poet and painter of invisible worlds and sacred places. She attended the New School for Social Research and Pratt in New York studying psychology, philosophy, comparative religions and art and graduated from the San Francisco Art Institute with degrees in Painting and Performance/Video. She trained with Multidimensional Research and Expansion for three years and later initiated a two year study on past life regression. Her visual and multi-media art speaks of inner worlds and unseen dimensions of reality.

Luminous has always had the ability to walk between the physical and spiritual worlds. Psychic phenomena, including several near death experiences, levitation, stigmata, a vast psychic and spiritual opening and incidents of spontaneous healing informed her directly and deeply of the limitless possibilities available to us.

She founded the Temple of X-Static Sound (1985) to further awareness of the uses of vibrational frequency (Tibetan bowls, bells, crystal bowls) and voice harmonics. She is the Founder and Director of the Spiritual Archaeology Society (501C3 pending) to support and preserve ancient wisdom and traditions and advance the practice of Spiritual Archaeology.

For the past 20 years, she has gratefully lived and thrived in the mystical beauty of Sedona, Arizona. She is a world-renowned Transformational Consultant and successful Real Estate Broker. Luminous conducts Spiritual Archaeology trainings in Sedona and on the unique journeys she leads to sacred places around the world.

IMAGES BY LUMINOUS

Red Pyramid

Cahokia Sunrise

Doorway of Light

Carnac, Brittany, France

Seeing

Breakthrough

Newgrange, Ireland

Cat who walks between the worlds

Stairway to the Stars

Jaguar passing through dimensions

Nature—a question of balance

Sedona Moonscape

Lifeforce of the Iris

Petroglyphs Southwest

Sedona Dawning

Images appearing in this book are available in limited edition (50), museum quality giclees. Contact the publisher for further information or visit the publisher's website:

www.SpiritualArchaeologyBook.com

SPIRITUAL ARCHAEOLOGY TRAININGS take place on journeys to sacred places with the author and in Sedona, Arizona. A schedule of upcoming trainings is available in the Events Calendar on the website.

www.PortalsofTranscendence.com

෪   ෪   ෪

The Spiritual Archaeology Society is being formed as a non-profit organization—501c (3)—to advance spiritual development through education and for the preservation of indigenous knowledge and wisdom. This organization offers Basic, Advanced and Masters Certification Programs in Spiritual Archaeology and small group pilgrimages to sacred places to establish a direct connection to the earth, cosmos and ancient wisdom.

If you care to donate, please send checks to:

Spriritual Archaeology Society
POB 670
Sedona, Az 86339

Or visit our website to make a Paypal contribution.

www.PortalsofTranscendence.com

You will receive a letter indicating your tax deductible contribution once our final approval for non-profit has been attained. Many thanks.

CPSIA information can be obtained at www.ICGtesting.com
Printed in the USA
LVOW011240230912

299876LV00002B/2/P

9 780983 996811